Anfield Maestros

The 50 Greatest
Liverpool players
since 1945

By Dean Hayes

First published in 2003

This book is copyright under the Berne Convention. All rights are reserved. Apart from any fair dealing for the purpose of private study, research, criticism or review, as permitted under the Copyright Act, 1956, no part of this publication may be reproduced, stored in a retrieval system, or transmitted, in any form or by any means, electronic, electrical, chemical, mechanical, optical, photocopying, recording or otherwise, without the prior permission of the copyright owner. Enquiries should be sent to the publishers at the undermentioned address:

EMPIRE PUBLICATIONS
1 Newton Street, Manchester M1 1HW
© Dean Hayes 2003

ISBN 1901746348

Photographs courtesy of Liverpool Echo & Lancashire Evening Post
Jacket design & Layout: Ashley Shaw
Edited by Ashley Shaw & Stuart Fish

Contents

Alan A'Court 6	Sammy Lee 58
John Aldridge 8	Billy Liddell 60
John Barnes 10	Alec Lindsay 62
Gerry Byrne 12	Terry McDermott 64
Ian Callaghan 14	Steve McMahon 66
Jimmy Case 16	Steve McManaman 68
Ray Clemence 18	Jimmy Melia 70
Kenny Dalglish 20	Gordon Milne 72
David Fairclough 22	Jan Molby 74
Robbie Fowler 24	Ronnie Moran 76
Steven Gerrard 26	Phil Neal 78
Bruce Grobbelaar 28	Steve Nicol 80
Alan Hansen 30	Michael Owen 82
Steve Heighway 32	Jamie Redknapp 84
Ray Houghton 34	Ian Rush 86
Emlyn Hughes 36	Tommy Smith 88
Roger Hunt 38	Graeme Souness 90
David Johnson 40	Ian St John 92
Craig Johnston 42	Peter Thompson 94
Rob Jones 44	Phil Thompson 96
Kevin Keegan 46	John Toshack 98
Alan Kennedy 48	Ronnie Whelan 100
Ray Kennedy 50	Mark Wright 102
Chris Lawler 52	Ron Yeats 104
Tommy Lawrence 54	Merseyside Derby 106
Mark Lawrenson 56	Empire Books 107

INTRODUCTION

Liverpool Football Club have, in the years since the Second World War, won every trophy the British and European game has to offer. Starting from the club's fifth league championship success in the first season after the war, the Anfield side have become the most successful club in English football.

Meanwhile, the players who have contributed to this success are among the greatest in the British game. Naturally the great 1970s and 80s team dominated initially by the skills of Keegan and Toshack and later Dalglish and Souness spring instantly to mind but what of the heroes of yesteryear: the Billy Liddells and Tommy Lawrences who endeared themselves to fans in the immediate postwar period.

Then there are the heroes of today, the Owens and Gerrards who have helped a resurgence at Anfield over the past few seasons, with the promise of a return to former glories.

However any such compilation is bound to be subjective. How could one compare a player of the 1940s and 1950s, when at times Liverpool were in the Second Division, with the standards in the top flight today? Football has changed dramatically, particularly with the influx of overseas players and the growth of the professional game. Most concede that today's game is faster and tougher than ever before.

Though this book offers a fascinating insight into a vast range of footballers who have played for the Reds there are controversial omissions such as David James, Larry Lloyd and Sami Hyypia to name but three. Therefore, I am sure the book will stimulate debate and argument over the selections made.

Dean P Hayes
Pembrokeshire
August 2002

ALAN A'COURT

Born	30 September 1934
Birthplace	Rainhill
Height	5ft 10ins
Weight	11st 10lbs

Team	Apps	Gls
Liverpool	355	61
Tranmere R	50	11

Alan A'Court caused something of a stir in his rugby-loving family when he chose soccer as his livelihood. He joined Liverpool on his eighteenth birthday and made his debut wearing the No. 9 shirt in February 1953 during the Reds 3-2 defeat of Middlesbrough. However, with Billy Liddell usually occupying his favoured left-flank position, the exciting youngster spent the next two seasons drifting in and out of the Liverpool side, getting a chance only when the Scottish international was injured or selected at centre-forward.

It was following the Reds' relegation to the Second Division that A'Court established himself as a regular in the Liverpool side. Yet despite the presence of two outstanding wingers in A'Court and Liddell, who by this time had switched to the other wing, the Reds continued to find it difficult to escape the Second Division.

After representing the Football League and making seven England Under-23 appearances, A'Court was capped by England, making his full international debut against Northern Ireland in 1957. The following year he made four further appearances, three of those in the 1958 World Cup Finals in Sweden. After that, like Bolton's Doug Holden, he lost out to the fast-emerging Bobby Charlton.

In full flight, Alan A'Court was a stirring sight. A lynchpin of the Liverpool side that struggled for promotion for eight seasons, he was instrumental in the club achieving their goal in 1961-62. A'Court liked nothing better than to reach the by-line and cross the ball for the waiting Liverpool strikers. Though he wasn't a prolific scorer, he netted a particularly spectacular effort in Liverpool's 4-3 win over Chelsea in the third round of the FA Cup in January 1962. Towards the end of the promotion-winning

> "A'Court was one of the most difficult customers to confront Second Division full-backs during the fifties."

season, the Reds found themselves 2-0 down against fellow high-flyers Leyton Orient at Brisbane Road with just ten minutes to go. Up stepped long-serving A'Court with a brace to save a point!

A'Court remained a regular in the Reds line-up for the first half of their initial season back in the top flight before giving way temporarily to Kevin Lewis. However following the emergence of Peter Thompson, Alan found himself squeezed out of the side completely, playing his final game for Liverpool against Reykjavik of Iceland in the second leg of a European Cup tie in September 1964.

On leaving Anfield, he saw out his playing days with Tramnere Rovers, scoring the winner on his debut as the Prenton Park club beat Stockport County 3-2. In February 1966 he netted his only hat-trick in the Football League as Tranmere beat Bradford City 4-2 at Valley Parade.

After hanging up his boots, he held various coaching jobs at Norwich, Chester, Crewe and Stoke as well as in Zambia.

Though he was unsuccessful in his bid to become an international star, it should not detract from his achievements for Alan A'Court was one of the most difficult customers to confront Second Division full-backs during the late fifties.

Honours:
2nd Div Championship 1961-62
5 England caps

JOHN ALDRIDGE

Born	18 September 1958
Birthplace	Liverpool
Height	5ft 11ins
Weight	12st 3lbs

Team	Apps	Gls
Newport Co.	159 (11)	69
Oxford United	111(3)	72
Liverpool	69(14)	50
Tranmere R	221(21)	138

A Liverpool fan since childhood, John Aldridge harboured an ambition to step down from the terraces of Anfield's Spion Kop to play for the Reds. After a trial as a 14-year-old he was told they would be in touch - but it took another 14 years for the phone to ring!

Aldridge began his career playing part-time for non-League South Liverpool before joining Newport County in April 1979, after finishing his apprenticeship as a British Leyland toolmaker. He won the Welsh Cup with Newport in 1980 but after five seasons at Somerton Park, he took his goalscoring touch to Oxford United in a £78,000 deal. He helped the Manor Ground side win promotion from Division Three to Division One in successive seasons and victory in the League Cup Final of 1986. In four seasons with Oxford, Aldridge scored 72 goals in 114 League and Cup games. When it became clear that Ian Rush would be joining Juventus, the way was finally clear for Aldridge to realise his dream and in January 1987 he joined Liverpool for £750,000.

'Aldo' flourished at Anfield where he had three highly successful seasons, scoring 61 goals in 103 League and Cup games. However it was in season 1987-88 when Aldridge hit the headlines, for after scoring in the opening nine League matches, his clinical finishing brought him 29 League and Cup goals. However, though he was a ferocious and accurate penalty-taker, he was completely devastated to miss in that season's FA Cup Final against Wimbledon, for not only was it his only miss for Liverpool but it robbed the Reds of a much-deserved double.

When Rush returned from Italy, it became obvious that Anfield was not big enough for both of them though 'Aldo' did net a hat-trick in a 3-0 win at Charlton Athletic while Rush spent most of his time in the Selhurst Park dugout. But at the end of that 1988/89 season,

Aldridge joined Spanish club Real Sociedad for £1.1 million.

His exploits in Spain earned him the nickname 'El Zorro' after he became the first Real player to score in six consecutive matches. After two years with the club, during which he scored 40 goals in 76 games, he returned to Merseyside, signing for John King's Tranmere Rovers for a bargain £250,000. In his first season at Prenton Park, Aldridge equalled Bunny Bell's record of 1933-34 by scoring 40 goals. He was the club's top scorer for six successive seasons before becoming Tranmere's player-manager in April 1996 following the departure of John King.

Though international honours eluded Aldridge until he was 27, when he finally made his debut against Wales in Jack Charlton's first match in charge, he became an integral part of the Irish set-up for a good number of years, going on to score 19 goals in 69 games, just one goal short of the Irish scoring record.

At the end of the 1997-98 season, John decided to concentrate fully on management following a Tranmere career in which he had scored 174 goals in 294 League and Cup. However despite taking Rovers to the 2000 League Cup Final against Leicester City, Aldridge later parted company with the Wirral club. Aldridge was a great favourite with the Kop and though he spent just three years at Anfield, his heart always belonged to the Reds.

Honours:
League Championship 1987-88
FA Cup 1988-89
69 Republic of Ireland caps

JOHN BARNES

Born	7 Novemeber 1963
Birthplace	Jamaica
Height	5ft 11ins
Weight	12st 7lbs

Team	Apps	Gls
Watford	232 (1)	65
Liverpool	310 (4)	84
Newcastle U	22 (4)	6
Charlton Ath.	2 (10)	0

Jamaican-born John Barnes came to live in England in 1976 when his father was posted to London as Jamaica's military attaché. John's attachment to football grew with every day and the following year, as his parents were about to return to Jamaica, he decided to remain in England and devote his life to the game.

While he was playing for Sudbury Court in the Middlesex League, Barnes' skills caught the eye of Watford director and former Arsenal manager Bertie Mee, who persuaded the 17-year-old to sign professional forms for the Vicarage Road club. After making his League debut against Oldham Athletic in September 1981, he helped the Hornets win promotion to Division One and was a member of the Watford side that lost to Everton in the 1984 FA Cup Final. For six successive seasons, his goalscoring reached double figures - the only player in Watford's history to achieve this feat.

In June 1987, after scoring 84 goals in 286 League and Cup games for Watford, Barnes joined Liverpool for a fee of £900,000. Of course he became an instant subject of controversy - Anfield was not a place where black players had previously flourished. However, he soon had the Liverpool faithful cheering him when - in only his second match against Oxford - he smashed home a spectacular goal of his own after laying one on for John Aldridge. The Liverpool fans nicknamed him 'Tarmac' - the black Heighway!

Barnes was a player renowned for his dazzling dribbling and finishing and less than twelve months after making his England debut against Northern Ireland, he confirmed his potential with a brilliant solo goal against Brazil in Rio de Janeiro. He ran through the entire Brazilian defence and dribbled round the goalkeeper to crack in the opening goal in England's 2-0 win in the Maracana - even the partisan Brazilians applauded the feat.

Although not a great goalscorer, Barnes was a scorer of great goals. He could score with his head or either foot, his speciality being his ability to bend a

again in 1990, joining an elite band of players who have won the award twice.

One of the most skilful players this country has ever produced, Barnes suffered a succession of niggling injuries before taking over the captaincy following Steve Nicol's decision to relinquish the job. Towards the end of his Anfield career, he switched positions to become the club's midfield anchor man, winning the ball in his own half and becoming the springboard for the attacks with his quick and accurate distribution.

In the summer of 1997 Bames was given a free transfer and joined former colleague Kenny Dalglish at Newcastle United where in his first season at St James' Park, he helped the Magpies reach the FA Cup Final. He later had a spell with Charlton Athletic before becoming part of the Celtic 'dream ticket' under Kenny Dalglish. Unfortunately for Barnes, who was awarded the MBE for his services to football, things didn't work out at Parkhead and he was replaced by Martin O'Neill.

ball at free-kicks with spectacular results - his stunning goal for England against Yugoslavia in Belgrade, where he beat a six-man defensive wall, being a prime example of this skill.

He also struck a brilliant goal against Arsenal in a televised match before netting his first Liverpool hat-trick against Coventry City in May 1990. He was voted Footballer of the Year in his first season at Anfield and won the honour

Honours
League Championship
1987-88, 1989-90
FA Cup 1988-89
79 England caps

GERRY BYRNE

Born	29 August 1938
Birthplace	Liverpool
Height	5ft 10ins
Weight	12st 6lbs

Team	Apps	Gls
Liverpool	273 (1)	2

When Bill Shankly arrived at Anfield in December 1959, the career of full-back Gerry Byrne was going nowhere. He had joined the staff in 1955 straight from school and had made just two first-team appearances, putting through his own goal on his debut - his performances for the club's Central League side were only moderate and he had been placed on the transfer list at his own request. In fact, Gerry Byme had the hallmark of a player who would be on the fringe of big-time football for a number of years before drifting towards a lower grade.

However, following an injury to Ronnie Moran, Gerry Byrne stepped in to give a series of accomplished performances and when Moran returned to first-team action, he kept his place by switching to right-back in place of Dick White.

"Shankly would later say, 'When Gerry went, it took a big chunk out of Liverpool. Something special was missing.'"

During the Reds' promotion-winning season of 1961-62, Byrne was an ever-present as Liverpool won the Second Division Championship, finishing eight points ahead of runners-up Leyton Orient.

Following the emergence of Chris Lawler, Byme reverted to left-back to replace the ageing Moran. Over the next seven seasons, Byrne proved himself to be one of the most reliable defenders in the First Division. Though he wasn't the quickest of Full-backs, he was one of the greatest readers of the game.

Ferocious in the tackle, his performance in the 4-0 aggregate defeat of Belgian champions Anderlecht in the 1964-65 European Cup competition was described by Shankly as 'the best full-back display Europe has ever seen'.

Gerry Byme's finest moment came

He was capped twice by England at full international level, though in the first of his two outings, he was given the run-around by Scotland's Willie Henderson.

At Anfield, Byrne was a member of the Liverpool side that won the League Championship in 1963-64 and 1965-66 but a knee injury sustained in a 3-2 win over Leicester City on the opening day of the 1966-67 season meant that he was never quite the same dominant force again.

Sadly, recurring knee trouble prompted the popular defender's premature retirement at Wembley in 1965 as the Reds met Leeds United in that season's FA Cup Final. He played for just under two hours with a broken collar bone, overcoming great pain and hiding his discomfort from Don Revie's side. It was Byrne who laid on Liverpool's first goal in extra-time when, taking an inch-perfect pass from Willie Stevenson, he reached the by-line before crossing the ball for Roger Hunt to head home.

Though he enjoyed success at club level, the Liverpool defender was less successful on the international front. in 1969, after which he joined the club's coaching staff for a while. Shanks was warm in his praise for one of the surest defenders in the top flight when he said: 'When Gerry went, it took a big chunk out of Liverpool. Something special was missing.'

Honours
League Championship
1963-64, 1965-66
Second Division Championship
1961-62
FA Cup 1964-65
2 England caps

IAN CALLAGHAN

Born	10 April 1942
Birthplace	Liverpool
Height	5ft 11ins
Weight	11st 1lbs

Team	Apps	Gls
Liverpool	637 (3)	50
Swansea City	76	1
Crewe Alex	15	0
Charlton Ath.	2 (10)	0

Ian Callaghan joined the Reds straight from school and made his League debut as a teenager in a 4-0 win over Bristol Rovers in April 1960 after just four outings in the club's Central League side. Yet it was another season and a half before he was given a regular spot in the Liverpool side as they won promotion to the First Division.

In the top flight, Callaghan's game blossomed. He was fast and direct, getting to the by-line to feed Hunt and St John with the type of crosses that brought the strikers plenty of goals. No great scorer himself, two of his efforts are worth recalling. Against Everton in 1963, his spectacular 30-yarder sunk the Blues as Liverpool headed for their first League Championship. Against Inter Milan in the 1965 European Cup semi-final at Anfield, he side-footed home from an acute angle after Stevenson and Hunt had worked a well-rehearsed free-kick routine.

Though on the small side and slightly built, Callaghan was a courageous and determined player. An old-fashioned winger, at Liverpool he was turned into a central midfield player - his appetite for the ball and work-rate being a great influence in the formative years under Bill Shankly. He only played four times for England, scant reward for such an outstanding club career. He played twice under Alf Ramsey in 1966 but it was eleven years before he added another cap to his collection when manager Ron Greenwood decided to try a block of seven Liverpool players in a friendly against Switzerland.

Callaghan was 35 when he played his last international game - the fact that he was even considered at that age speaks volumes for his fitness and durability. Ian Callaghan was not a player to grab the headlines but one who always gave a fully committed performance for the ninety minutes. He had a tremendous standard of dedication, loyalty and skill, embodying the qualities that built Liverpool into possibly the greatest club side in the world.

He won five League Championship medals, one Second Division Championship medal, two FA Cup winners' medals, two UEFA Cup winners' medals and a European Cup winners' medal. In 1974 he was voted Footballer of the Year. Liverpool's longest-serving player, the last of Ian's 848 appearances for the Reds was on 29 March 1978 - a European Cup semi-final first leg against Borussia Moenchengladbach. On leaving Liverpool, Callaghan went to Swansea where he helped his old team-mate John Toshack lift the Swans out of the Third Division. After leaving Vetch Field he had spells with Cork Hibernian and Soudifjord of Norway before ending his illustrious career with Crewe Alexandra. Never cautioned by a referee, Ian Callaghan was deserving of the MBE awarded to him for his services to football.

League Championship
1963-64, 1965-66
1972-73 1975-76 1976-77
Second Division Championship
1961-62
FA Cup 1964-65 1973-74
European Cup 1976-77
UEFA Cup 1972-73 1975-76
4 England caps

JIMMY CASE

Born	18 May 1954
Birthplace	Liverpool
Height	5ft 9ins
Weight	12st 12lbs

Team	Apps	Gls
Liverpool	170 (16)	23
Brighton HA	154 (5)	10
Southampton	213 (2)	10
Bournemouth	38 (2)	1
Halifax Town	17 (4)	2
Wrexham	1 (3)	0
Darlington	1	0

Like Steve Heighway, Jimmy Case was plucked from local football, signing for the Reds from non-League South Liverpool in 1973. He had to wait almost two years before making his League debut against Queen's Park Rangers in April 1975 in an attacking role wide on the right. However, it was midway through the 1975-76 season before Case's explosive talents earned him a regular spot in the Liverpool side at the expense of midfielder Bran Hall.

Though not a prolific goalscorer, he netted a stunning hat-trick in a 3-0 win over Slask Wroclaw of Poland, a UEFA Cup game played in 15 degrees of frost. The Reds went on to reach the final of that season's UEFA Cup where their opponents were FC Bruges. Case had been left out of the first leg at Anfield but with the Reds two down, he came on as substitute for John Toshack. A series of rampaging runs down the right flank unsettled the previously calm Belgians as Case inspired a typical Anfield comeback - the Reds winning 3-2 with Jimmy netting the equaliser himself. As if that wasn't sufficient he ended his first full season with League Championship and UEFA Cup winners' medals.

In 1976-77 Case found himself in competition with Terry McDermott for one of he midfield positions but as the Reds treble-hunting campaign drew to a conclusion, it was Case who wore the No. 8 shirt. He played an enterprising part in the club's League and European Cup triumphs, while he was the Reds' best player in the FA Cup Final against Manchester United, scoring Liverpool's goal in a 2-1 defeat.

Capped by England at Under-23 level, he never represented his country at senior level but what he missed in international football he more than made up for with a clutch of other honours - three European Cup medals, four League Championship medals and a UEFA Cup medal.

Midway through the 1980-81 season, Case lost his place to the industrious Sammy Lee and at the end of the season, he signed for former Liverpool star Jimmy Melia at Brighton and Hove Albion for a fee of £350,000. During his second season with the Seagulls, he had the huge satisfaction of returning to Anfield to score the goal that knocked his former team-mates out of the FA Cup. Brighton went on to reach the final but went down 4-0 to Manchester United after the first game had ended all-square at 2-2.

Case later moved down the coast to Southampton as a replacement for Steve Williams and soon showed that he had lost none of his tenacity. Blossoming in the play-maker's role denied him at Anfield by the majestic Graeme Souness, it could just be that he was allowed to leave Liverpool too soon.

Case left the Dell in the summer of 1991 to play for Bournemouth.

He later had spells with Halifax Town, Wrexham and Darlington before returning to Brighton for an ill-fated spell as player-manager. He then continued his managerial apprenticeship, taking over the reins at Dr Marten's League side, Bashley.

Honours
League Championship
1975-76, 1976-77 1978-79 1979-80
Football League Cup 1980-81
European Cup
1976-77, 1977-78, 1980-81
UEFA Cup 1975-76

RAY CLEMENCE

Born	5 August 1948
Birthplace	Skegness
Height	6ft 0ins
Weight	12st 9lbs

Team	Apps	Gls
Scunthorpe U	48	0
Liverpool	470	0
Tottenham H	240	0

It was Bill Shankly who paid Scunthorpe United £18,000 for the 19-year-old Ray Clemence who had made 48 appearances for the Irons in the lower divisions. Shankly's assessment of the man was that he was possibly the most important factor in Liverpool's continued success throughout the seventies. Indeed, Clemence only missed six matches during that period.

Clemence had to wait two-and-a-half seasons before clinching a place in the Reds' first team as Tommy Lawrence's consistent form kept him out. But he immediately impressed with safe handling and sharp reflexes. He got down quickly to low shots, knew when not to come off his line and had great positional sense. In his first full season, he conceded only 22 goals in 41 games, helping the Reds equal the First Division record of 24 in a season. In 1978-79 he was even better, letting in only 16 goals.

Of course, being behind one of the world's best defences, he needed to have great powers of concentration. He was kept idle for long periods, not getting a touch of the ball. It was a measure of his greatness that when he did have to respond, he would produce a top-class save. Of lightweight build and very athletic, he was able to spring several feet into the air and claim the ball with a very safe pair of hands. He was also one of the first goalkeepers to act as a sweeper behind his defence, leaving his penalty area to cut out the long through ball.

His world-class saves were many but perhaps there were none more important than in the 1975-76 UEFA Cup away leg at Dynamo Dresden. He saved a penalty by diving full length to his right to reach a hard low shot and keep the tie goalless after ninety minutes.

One of the finest goalkeepers in the history of the game, he was unlucky to be around at the same time as Peter Shilton, for throughout his illustrious career at international level, in which he won 61 caps, he was always vying for the No.1 jersey with Shilts.

In August 1981 Clemence announced that he was looking for a new challenge and although he was still at the top of his game he moved to Spurs. He had hardly missed a match throughout his time at Anfield and picked up more club honours than any other goalkeeper, as well as holding the record for consecutive first team appearances by an English goalkeeper - 325.

Clemence made his Spurs' debut in the 1981 FA Charity Shield and in his first season at White Hart Lane he helped the club retain the FA Cup and reach the League Cup Final where they lost to Liverpool. Shortly after appearing in the 1987 FA Cup Final injuries began to affect his high level of performance and he was forced to retire.

After being appointed goalkeeping coach at Spurs, Ray had a spell as manager of Barnet before becoming England's full-time goalkeeping coach.

Possibly the best goalkeeper Liverpool have ever had, Clemence's 23 seasons brought him five League Championship medals, five FA Cup Final appearances, three European Cup winners' medals and an MBE in the Queen's Birthday Honours for services to football.

Honours
League Championship
1972-73, 1975-76;
1976-77;1978-79;1979-80;
FA Cup 1973-74
League Cup 1980-81
European Cup
1976-77; 1977-78; 1980-81;
UEFA Cup 1972-73; 1975-76;
61 England caps

KENNY DALGLISH

Born	4 March 1951
Birthplace	Glasgow
Height	5ft 8ins
Weight	11st 13 lbs

Team	Apps	Gls
Liverpool	342 (13)	118

Brought up in the shadow of Ibrox Park, Kenny Dalglish was always expected to play in the blue of Rangers and not the green and white hoops. But it was Celtic who signed him. When their assistant-manager Sean Fallon went to meet the family, the young Dalglish rushed around in panic, ripping the Rangers pictures off the wall of the living room!

In his first full season with Celtic, Dalglish scored 17 goals and made his international debut as a substitute in Scotland's 1-0 win over Belgium in 1971. His skills were subtle and stemmed from the balance and speed with which he controlled the ball. His passing was immaculate and his deceptive swirls in full flight would often send defenders the wrong way.

In eight years with Celtic, Dalglish won five League titles, four Scottish Cups and a Scottish Cup winners' medal. In his final season at Parkhead, he led Celtic to yet another League and Cup double, this time as captain. Celtic manager Jock Stein recognised Dalglish's all-round skills and assigned him to midfield where he still continued to score memorable goals. But at the age of 26 Dalglish wanted to prove himself in England and in 1977 Liverpool signed him for £440,000, manager Bob Paisley citing the player's 'attitude' as a key attribute - his dedication, professionalism and determination to succeed.

Dalglish made a quiet start in the Charity Shield against Manchester United but scored on his League debut at Middlesbrough. He ended his first season at Anfield as top scorer as Liverpool stormed to the League title again and Dalglish was voted Footballer of the Year. After joining Liverpool, he made 177 consecutive League and Cup appearances before missing his first game in 1980. That was the year he picked up another European Cup winners' medal and Liverpool retained their League title.

He had been instrumental in Liverpool winning the 1978 European Cup Final against Bruges, scoring the only goal of the game. He played in the World Cup Finals of 1974, 1978 and 1982, scoring the equaliser in Scotland's famous 3-2 win over Holland in Argentina in 1978.

Liverpool continued to dominate British football and Dalglish remained the key figure. In 1983 he scored his 100th goal for the Reds to become only the third player ever to score a century of goals in both Scottish and English football. He was voted Footballer of the Year again and picked up the players' Player of the Year award as Liverpool won their fourteenth League Championship.

Following the Heysel Stadium tragedy in 1985, Dalglish was appointed successor to Joe Fagan as Liverpool's player-manager. His first season in charge could not have been more successful. Liverpool became only the third club in the twentieth century to complete the League and FA Cup double with Kenny's goal at Stamford Bridge clinching the title. Not only did Dalglish win the Manager of the Year award but he also collected his 100th cap and he continued to have great success at Anfield until 22 February 1991 when he rocked the soccer world by resigning, citing the pressures of the job.

Blackburn Rovers ended his self-imposed exile and after spending some of the money that Jack Walker had made available to him, Dalglish led the club to the play-offs and Premiership football. In 1993-94, Rovers finished runners-up to Manchester United but the following season won the Premier League title in style despite a final day defeat at Anfield. Kenny then stepped down to become the club's Director of Football but later announced his departure from Ewood Park. After a spell in charge at Newcastle United he returned to Parkhead as Director of Football Operations but left the club following the appointment of Martin O'Neill.

Honours
League Championship
1978-79, 1979-80, 1981-82,
1982-83, 1983-84, 1985-86,
FA Cup 1985-86
League Cup
1980-81, 1981-82,
1982-83, 1983-84
European Cup
1977-78, 1980-81, 1983-84
102 Scotland caps

DAVID FAIRCLOUGH

Born	5 January 1957
Birthplace	Liverpool
Height	6ft 1ins
Weight	12st 6 lbs

Team	Apps	Gls
Liverpool	64 (34)	34
Norwich City	1 (1)	0
Oldham Ath.	6 (11)	1
Tranmere R	3 (11)	1
Wigan Ath.	4 (3)	1

Better known as 'Super Sub', there is no doubt that David Fairclough was at his most effective in the No 12 shirt. Though he made his League debut in November 1975, he caused his first sensation the following spring when his goals turned the title race in Liverpool's favour. Coming on as substitute, he won the points in the games at Anfield against Burnley, Stoke City and Everton - his winner against the Blues coming in the final minute of the game. Fairclough also started a number of games, netting at both Carrow Road and Maine Road.

Tall, gangly and carrot-haired, avid Fairclough was unmistakable. He was quick and dangerous, prepared to run at defences and carry the ball into the penalty area. It was very difficult to shake him off the ball and he had the knack of being in the right scoring place at the right time.

In the following season's European Cup quarter-final against St Etienne at Anfield, the French side held the advantage of an away goal when Fairclough replaced John Toshack. Five minutes from time, he received a pass from Ray Kennedy and dribbled past three defenders before slipping the ball under the advancing keeper to put the Reds into the semi-finals. After that, Bob Paisley began to name him in his starting line-up with more frequency.

However, despite his many attributes, Fairclough really had only one season as a Liverpool regular. That was 1977-78, when he ended the campaign with a European Cup winners' medal - a personal highlight in his career.

Sadly, Fairclough's overall form was patchy and in the games that he did start, he had a tendency to drift out of the action, seeming to lack both stamina and concentration. As new players began to arrive at Anfield, he began to slip out of contention but even when he did return to the side for the odd game, he continued to frustrate a section of the Liverpool crowd - one minute displaying a gloriously unexpected touch, the next fluffing the simplest of passes.

On leaving the Reds, he went to Canada to play for Toronto Blizzards before playing for Swiss club Lucerne. On his return to England he turned out for Norwich City and Oldham Athletic before joining Belgian club Beveren SK.

In August 1989 he joined Tranmere Rovers but after just one season at Prenton Park, in which he failed to establish himself as a first team regular, he signed for Wigan Athletic. Injuries restricted his appearances and he was forced to hang up his boots. Though he will go down as a man of whom the public expected too much, Fairclough will always be remembered for the major role he played in Liverpool's assault on Europe.

David Fairclough is now a freelance journalist, having successfully completed a course for the National Council for Training Journalists during his playing days.

Honours
League Championship
1975-76, 1976-77, 1979-80
European Cup 1977-78;
UEFA Cup 1975-76

ROBBIE FOWLER

Born	9 April 1975
Birthplace	Liverpool
Height	5ft 10ins
Weight	12st 3 lbs

Team	Apps	Gls
Liverpool	209 (27)	120
Leeds Utd	22	12
Manchester C.	12 (1)	2

Robbie Fowler grew up an Everton fan but made the transition from the Goodison terraces to the Anfield playing staff because the Reds were quicker to recognise his obvious talent for scoring goals.

As an 18-year-old, Fowler scored on his debut in the League Cup at Fulham and followed this up in the Anfield return by becoming the first Liverpool player to score five times in a game since Ian Rush achieved the feat a decade earlier. He opened his League account at only the third time of asking and fired his first Premiership hat-trick just two matches later as the Reds beat Southampton 4-2. He began his first full season by netting the fastest hat-trick in Premiership history as Arsenal were beaten 3-0 and ended by breaking the 30-goal barrier and picking up a League Cup winners' medal.

In 1995-96, Fowler scored four goals against Bolton Wanderers on his way to another best-ever total of 35 goals from 53 games and only an FA Cup Final blank prevented him from becoming the first player to score in every round since Peter Osgood in 1970.

Fowler went on to score his first international goal the following term, and another four against Middlesbrough in December 1996 saw him reach the milestone of 100 goals for Liverpool in 165 matches - one match fewer than Ian Rush had taken! He finished the season with 31 goals and might have beaten his previous best had he not missed five games through injury and been ruled out of the last three games of the season after being sent off against Everton.

As in previous seasons, Fowler's goals in 1997-98 were vital to the cause, his ability to be in the right place at the right time offered him more goalscoring opportunities than the majority of other strikers in the game. Sadly, he picked up a knee injury in the game against Everton at Anfield in February

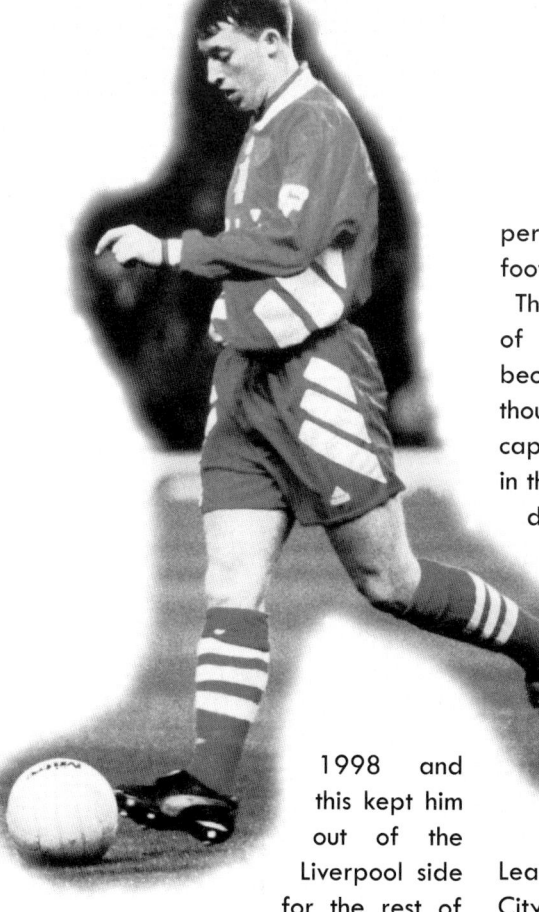

1998 and this kept him out of the Liverpool side for the rest of the campaign.

He returned to action as strike partner to Michael Owen early the following season and scored twice in a 3-3 draw against Charlton Athletic. A superb hat-trick against Southampton in a 7-1 victory earned him the 'Man of the Match' award but thereafter his season declined as he proceeded to shoot himself in the foot with some extraordinary examples of well-documented behaviour in which he appeared to have allowed his personal views to get in the way of his footballing talent.

The 1999-2000 season was one of great disappointment for Fowler because of a spate of injuries and though he won five more international caps for England, contributing a goal in the 2-0 victory over the Ukraine, he didn't feature during the Euro 2000 tournament although he was selected for the final 22.

Fowler had to sit on the bench for two of the three finals that the Reds won in 2000-01 but capped a great season by scoring Liverpool's goal in the League Cup Final against Birmingham City. Latching on to a flick-on from Emile Heskey, he fired a superb dipping volley into the roof of the net.

During the close season, there were many rumours about Robbie Fowler's future and though the England forward pledged his future to the cup treble winners, he left Anfield to join the Reds' Premiership rivals, Leeds United.

Honours
FA Cup 2000-01
League Cup 1994-95, 2000-01
UEFA Cup 2000-01
15 England caps

STEVEN GERRARD

Born	30 May 1980
Birthplace	Liverpool
Height	6ft 2ins
Weight	12st 4 lbs

Team	Apps	Gls
Liverpool	119 (17)	16

An outstanding Anfield talent, Steven Gerrard made his full Liverpool first team debut in the centre of midfield at Tottenham Hotspur in December 1998 after a series of excellent displays in the club's reserve side. Though the Reds lost that game 2-1, Gerrard impressed with his strong tackling and penetrating through balls to strikers Fowler and Owen.

Though two-thirds of his appearances in 1998-99 were as a substitute, Gerrard started Liverpool's second round second leg UEFA Cup tie against Celta Vigo and though the Spanish outfit went through 4-1 on aggregate, Gerrard was named 'Man of the Match'.

He was invited to train with Kevin Keegan's England team in March 1999 but on his return to Anfield he received a scare when he was diagnosed with a stress fracture at the base of his back. Thankfully after several tests, he was given the all-clear and named as substitute for the 160th Merseyside derby at Anfield. Though the Blues took the lead through Oliver Dacourt after only 40 seconds, the Reds hit back to lead 3-1 through two goals by Robbie Fowler and another from Michael Owen. Francis Jeffers volleyed past David James to reduce the arrears and then twice in the last three minutes, Steven Gerrard cleared shots off the line from Danny Cadamarteri. The second Gerrard clearance was the last kick of the game!

It was 1999-2000 when Steven Gerrard established himself as a first team regular. He had an excellent season, culminating in winning full international honours against the Ukraine in May. Gerrard had already captained England Under-18s and scored on his Under-21 debut against Luxembourg but his composure in the senior game was a revelation, so much so that he forced his way into Kevin Keegan's final 22 for the European Championship Finals when he appeared as a substitute against Germany.

Gerrard's first Football League goal came at home in the 4-1 win over Sheffield Wednesday in December 1999 and what a goal it was. Having started the move deep in his own half, he picked the ball up again from Roberto Song about 60 yards from goal. After waltzing through the Wednesday midfield, he found himself confronted by the Owls' defence. A drop of the shoulder sent former England international Des Walker the wrong way before Gerrard shot past Kevin Pressman from an acute angle.

Though the on-going problem with his back re-emerged in the 2000-01 season and he paid a number of visits to his specialist in France for treatment, the Liverpool midfielder had a magnificent season. He was fit enough to play in six games in nineteen days as the Reds completed their season of Cup glory, even scoring Liverpool's second goal in the 5-4 defeat of Alaves to win the UEFA Cup.

Tagged England's latter-day Bryan Robson, Gerrard, who scored one

of England's goals in the 5-1 win in Germany, is fast developing into a key component in Sven Goran-Eriksson's line-up and his absence through injury from the 2002 World Cup had a detrimental effect on the national side's chances.

Now much more confident of his own fitness and ability to extend himself for a full ninety minutes, Steven is being touted as the next decade's best midfielder.

Honours
FA Cup 2000-01
League Cup 2000-01, 2002-03
UEFA Cup 2000-01
18 England caps

BRUCE GROBBELAAR

Born	6 October 1957
Birthplace	Durban, S. Africa
Height	6ft 1ins
Weight	14st 2 lbs

Team	Apps	Gls
Crewe Alex.	24	1
Liverpool	440	0
Stoke City (L)	4	0
Southampton	32	0
Plymouth A	36	0
Oldham A	4	0
Bury	1	0
Lincoln City	2	0

Goalkeeper Bruce Grobbelaar served in the Zimbabwean Army during the civil war before seeking a football career abroad, firstly with Vancouver Whitecaps in the North American Soccer League. He had a spell as a non-contract player with Crewe Alexandra, making his Football League debut against Wigan Athletic in December 1979. He became the club's regular keeper, playing on to the end of the season and actually scoring from the spot against York City in his last game for the club before returning to Vancouver. A year later, Bob Paisley brought him to Anfield as understudy to Ray Clemence.

However, after Clemence's mysterious departure to Tottenham Hotspur, Grobbelaar found himself the club's first-choice keeper and made his debut at Wolverhampton Wanderers on the opening day of the 1981-82 season. That first season he was an ever-present as Liverpool completed a League Championship - League Cup double.

The Kop loved his stunning saves, his sharp reflexes and the way he dominated the penalty area. In his first three seasons with the club, he won three League Championship winners' medals. In 1984 Liverpool won their fourth European Cup beating AS Roma in a penalty shoot-out, during which Grobbelaar even found time to perform a 'knobbly-knees' routine, much to the delight of the Liverpool fans. But the following year's European Cup Final was overshadowed by the Heysel Stadium tragedy, at which point Grobbelaar considered giving up football.

One of the highlights of Grobbelaar's career was the 1985-86 double season when once again he didn't miss a game. After a bout of meningitis

at the start of the 1988-89 season he won his place back from Mike Hooper as the side went 22 games undefeated.

He went through the similar heart-searching he'd gone through after Heysel following the Hillsborough disaster of 1989. At the subsequent inquiry into the semi-final tragedy, it was revealed that Grobbelaar saved many lives by insisting that the police let fans on to the pitch before more were killed in the crush behind his goal. His decision to continue playing was rewarded when Liverpool beat Everton 3-2 in the 1989 FA Cup Final. However, eventually his place in the team came under threat from both Mike Hooper and David James and in March 1993 he was loaned out to Stoke City.

An entertainer, extrovert in the extreme, he was a member of a Liverpool side that won six League Championships, three FA Cup trophies, four League Cups, the European Cup and the Super Cup.

On leaving Anfield in the summer of 1994, Grobbelaar joined Southampton on a free transfer, using his vast experience to bolster a young defence. In the home game against Everton he collided with Francis Benali, leaving him with a severe facial injury.

Eventually the strain of much-publicised events appeared to tell and he lost his place to Dave Beasant. His off-the-field problems restricted his appearances and he moved on to Plymouth Argyle. Despite some excellent performances for the Pilgrims, he was freed and in December 1997 he arrived at Oldham Athletic. After a handful of appearances he moved to Bury where, at 40 years 337 days, he became the Shakers' oldest player. He ended his career with Lincoln City.

Honours
League Championship
1981-81, 1982-83, 1983-84, 1985-86, 1987-88, 1989-90
FA Cup 1985-86, 1988-89, 1991-92
European Cup 1983-84
20 Zimbabwe cap

ALAN HANSEN

Born	13 June 1955
Birthplace	Alloa
Height	6ft 1ins
Weight	13st 0 lbs

Team	Apps	Gls
Liverpool	434	8

A multi-talented sportsman as a youngster, Alan Hansen was also an above-average scholar, leaving Lornshill Academy with seven 'O' levels and four 'A' levels. He had represented Scotland at golf, squash and volleyball but it was at football that he excelled. He'd actually had a trial with Liverpool when he was 15 but had been turned down. However, six years later, the Reds changed their minds and Bob Paisley paid Partick Thistle £100,000 for him in April 1977, by which time he had played 100 games for the Scottish League side.

Alan Hansen was arguably Bob Paisley's best-ever signing. He was an inspired long-term investment as was evident when he made his debut on 24 September 1977 in a 1-0 victory against Derby County, replacing the injured Phil Thompson. The Anfield crowd were used to the uncompromising play of Ron Yeats and Tommy Smith but Hansen's ability on the ball marked him out as a player of the highest class. His runs forward from defence as he accelerated past people as smoothly as a Rolls-Royce gave Liverpool's attacks an extra dimension. As an orthodox centre-half, he had few peers; his excellent reading of the game was supported by firm tackling and more-than-adequate ability in the air.

Making his international debut in 1979 and playing in the 1982 World Cup tournament, Hansen's failure to win more than 26 Scottish caps was a great mystery. He was even omitted from the 1986 World Cup party by Alex Ferguson. His constant rejection by his country's national team selectors may well go down as one of the greatest blunders in Scottish football. He surely would have been a permanent fixture in any other national side of the modern era.

"His runs forward from defence as he accelerated past people as smoothly as a Rolls-Royce gave Liverpool's attacks an extra dimension."

possessed the ability to make time and space to use the ball effectively. He set up John Aldridge's goal against Manchester United in November 1987 with a beautifully chipped pass to Steve McMahon who put the Reds' striker in.

However he realised during the 1988-89 season, during a lengthy lay-off, that the knee trouble he had suffered throughout his career was going to limit his appearances. So it came as no surprise to learn during the following season that he was retiring from the game.

One of TV's top soccer pundits, Alan Hansen displayed a record of consistency and quality that established him as one of the most outstanding post-war defenders and set him alongside the greatest names in Liverpool's glittering modern history.

Hansen replaced Phil Neal as captain in October 1985 and it was his leadership that played a vital part in the Reds' League and Cup double that season. It was probably the greatest moment in his illustrious career, for he became one of only five captains in the history of the game to lift the Championship trophy and the FA Cup in the same season. No matter who he partnered in the centre of the Reds' defence - Thompson, Lawrenson, Gillespie or Hysen - he thrived.

The most flourishing alliance was the superb partnership he formed with Republic of Ireland international Mark Lawrenson until the latter was forced to retire in 1987. Hansen

Honours
League Championship
1978-79, 1979-80, 1981-82, 1982-83, 1983-84, 1985-86, 1987-88, 1989-90
FA Cup 1985-86, 1988-89
League Cup 1980-81, 1982-83, 1983-84
European Cup 1977-78, 1980-81, 1983-84
26 Scotland caps

STEVE HEIGHWAY

Born	25 November 1947
Birthplace	Dublin
Height	5ft 11ins
Weight	11st 7 lbs

Team	Apps	Gls
Liverpool	312 (17)	50

Steve Heighway, who was born in Dublin, did not see a game of football until he moved to England with his parents at the age of ten. He was with Manchester City when he was 17 and although they gave him every opportunity to enjoy a footballer's life, his education always came first. He had done well at school - well enough that he eventually won a place at Warwick University.

Even at 21, when most footballers already have five years of full-time career behind them, Steve Heighway wasn't contemplating turning professional, never mind becoming part of one of the world's most successful teams. Fortunately soccer has a good scouting system and if you're any good, they'll catch you at any age.

Heighway was playing for Skelmersdale United, the club that was earning a growing reputation in the old Amateur Cup when he was caught and within weeks he was in the Liverpool first team. In September 1970 he made his international debut for the Republic of Ireland side against Poland in Dublin before he'd played in the Liverpool League side.

Heighway brought pace and width to the Liverpool attack, having a two-footed talent which enabled him to cut inside opponents or to pass them on the outside. In the months following his first-team debut, he turned the tide in the Merseyside derby with Liverpool 2-0 down. He scored the first from an acute angle and then provided the cross for John Toshack to equalise before Chris Lawler hit the winner. He ended his first campaign with a near post shot that deceived Arsenal keeper Bob Wilson to gave Liverpool the lead in the 1971 FA Cup Final that the Gunners later came back to win.

By the mid-1970s Heighway had become one of Liverpool's most consistent performers, spending much of his time in deep-lying positions and prompting the success of the Keegan-Toshack partnership.

Despite wearing the No 9 shirt, Heighway was a winger with the audacity to take on defenders and confound them, running at them and getting past them time and time again. Occasionally he over-elaborated but his ability to cross the ball at full speed gave the Reds a new dimension to their attacking play. His cross for Terry McDermott to head home in such style against Spurs in September 1978 was a prime example

Heighway's main task with Liverpool had been to penetrate on the flanks but he was a constant factor in a forward line that often opted to do without an orthodox centre-forward.

At the close of the decade, he crossed the Atlantic to end his playing days with Minnesota Kicks. After three seasons he became a coach, guiding the American Under-19 team to the last sixteen of the Junior World Cup. When the position of youth development officer at Anfield became available in 1988, he jumped at the chance to return to his spiritual home. He later became youth team manager and led his young charges to success in the FA Youth Cup in 1996.

According to Bill Shankly, Heighway, who picked up practically every honour the game has to offer, was 'an individualist who could win a match with one flash of genius'.

Honours
League Championship
1972-73, 1975-76, 1976-77, 1978-79
FA Cup 1973-74
UEFA Cup 1972-73, 1975-76
European Cup 1976-77, 1977-78,
34 Republic Of Ireland Caps

RAY HOUGHTON

Born	9 January 1962
Birthplace	Glasgow
Height	5ft 7 ins
Weight	10 st 10 lbs

Team	Apps	Gls
West Ham	0 (1)	0
Fulham	129 (16)	16
Oxford Utd	83	10
Liverpool	147 (6)	28
Aston Villa	69 (3)	7
Crystal Palace	69 (3)	7
Reading	33 (10)	1

Industrious midfielder Ray Houghton began his League career with West Ham United, making his debut as a substitute at Arsenal in May 1982. That was the only chance he got at Upton Park and after being released by John Lyall, he joined Fulham. An ever-present in his first season at Craven Cottage, he graced Fulham's side for three seasons before Oxford United, who were then in the top flight, paid £125,000 for his services. The Manor Ground club went on to win the League Cup, Houghton scoring the second goal in a 3-0 win over Queen's Park Rangers. Also in his first season with Oxford United, the Scotsman, who elected to represent the Republic of Ireland, his father's country of birth, won the first of 73 full caps.

In October 1987 Houghton joined Liverpool, his value having soared to £825,000. He made an instant impact on his debut but the game against

Norwich City ended goalless. The Kop soon warmed to him however as he created a series of chances for the forwards with his busy runs and accurate crosses and as the weeks passed it became obvious that Kenny Dalglish had made yet another astute signing. The player netted a number of vital goals including a header that helped the Reds beat Everton and a mid-air sidefooted volley against Manchester City at Maine Road - both in the FA Cup. After ending his first season at Anfield with a League Championship winners' medal, Houghton joined team-mates John Aldridge and Ronnie Whelan in the Republic of Ireland side for the 1988 European Championships. His performances at international level prompted the interest of a number of Italian clubs but Dalglish refused to part with him. He was in outstanding form in 1988-89 being an ever-present in the Liverpool side which narrowly failed to take the League title but won the FA Cup beating Everton 3-2 in the final.

Sadly, injuries caused Houghton to miss much of the 1989-90 season but he bounced back towards the end of the campaign to help the Liverpool cause. In 1991-92, his last season at Anfield, the Liverpool side were dogged by injury but Houghton held them together with his enthusiasm and determination. Unfortunately, he did not seem to figure in Graeme Souness' plans, possibly because of the restriction on international players and he was surprisingly sold to Aston Villa during the summer of 1992 for a little under £1 million.

Linking up with Andy Townsend and former Red Steve Staunton, both fellow Republic of Ireland internationals, Houghton helped Villa win the League Cup before returning to London to play for Crystal Palace. Though he could not prevent the Eagles slide from the Premiership, his combination of experience and energy proved vital as Palace regained top-flight status via the 1997 play-offs.

In the close season he joined Reading on a free transfer as player-coach but following the appointment as manager of Tommy Burns, who brought in his own coaching staff, Houghton left the Royals where he was much respected for his long and distinguished career in the game.

Honours
League Championship
1987-88, 1989-90
FA Cup 1988-89, 1991-92
73 Republic Of Ireland Caps

EMLYN HUGHES

Born	28 August 1947
Birthplace	Barrow
Height	5ft 10 ins
Weight	12 st 6 lbs

Team	Apps	Gls
Blackpool	27 (1)	0
Liverpool	474	35
Wolves	56 (2)	2
Rotherham U	55 (1)	6
Hull City	9	0
Swansea City	7	0
Reading	33 (10)	1

The son of a Welsh Rugby League star, Emlyn Hughes decided that the round ball game was better suited to his talents. He began his career with Blackpool, making his debut for the Seasiders against Blackburn Rovers in May 1966 as an 18-year-old. Liverpool manager Bill Shankly was watching the game and made an offer straight after the match but had to wait ten months before making his signing for £65,000.

Shanks predicted that, one day, Emlyn Hughes would lead England and of course he was right. He was a natural for the job, his unbounding energy and infectious enthusiasm helping him to collect 62 caps.

Emlyn arrived at Anfield in February 1967, making his debut against Stoke City, dominating ex-Arsenal and Newcastle United inside-forward George Eastham. A few matches later he brought down Newcastle forward Albert Bennett with a rugby tackle and was branded 'Crazy Horse' by the Kop - a nickname that he will keep forever.

Hughes made a few appearances at left-back for the injured Gerry Byrne but it was at left-half, replacing Willie Stevenson for the 1967-68 season, that he made a permanent position. Though he played on the left side and was good with both feet, he was stronger on his right. His dynamic surges into the opposition's penalty box brought him a fair share of spectacular goals. One of these came against Southampton at Anfield in April 1971 when after picking up the ball just outside his own area, he played it wide, stormed up the centre of the park to receive the return ball before cracking home an unstoppable shot from the edge of the Saints' box.

Hughes holds the record for the highest number of first-class matches

Loved by the Anfield crowd, he was voted Footballer of the Year in 1978 and won more international caps as a Liverpool player than anyone else.

In August 1979, having made 657 appearances in the famous red shirt, Hughes moved to Wolverhampton Wanderers. It came as no surprise when later that season they beat Nottingham Forest 1-0 at Wembley in the League Cup - it was the only club trophy Hughes needed to add to his collection. However Emlyn began to suffer with knee trouble during his stay at Wolves and moved into the lower divisions initially as player-manager with Rotherham United before playing for Hull City and Swansea.

An influential figure on the field during his successful years with Liverpool and England, Hughes' personality later earned him a nationwide reputation as a television celebrity.

in which any player has appeared in one season, when in 1972-73 he appeared 74 times for Liverpool! A versatile player, in 1973-74 he moved to the centre of the Reds' defence and replaced Tommy Smith as captain and though perhaps he wasn't as popular as Tommy, he was a great motivator and led by example. In his five seasons as captain, Hughes led Liverpool to two League Championships, two European Cups, the FA Cup and the UEFA Cup.

Honours
League Championship
1972-73, 1975-76,
1976-77, 1978-79
FA Cup 1973-74
European Cup
1976-77, 1977-78
UEFA Cup 1972-73, 1975-76
62 England caps

ROGER HUNT

Born	20 July 1938
Birthplace	Golborne
Height	5ft 9 ins
Weight	11 st 10 lbs

Team	Apps	Gls
Liverpool	401 (3)	245
Bolton W.	72 (4)	24

Spotted by former Liverpool and England centre-half Bill Jones, Roger Hunt had trials with Bury and Crewe before Liverpool signed him from Stockton Heath on amateur forms in 1958. He turned professional after completing his National Service and made his League debut as a 21-year-old against Scunthorpe United in September 1959, scoring in a 2-0 win. He quickly secured a regular place, netting 21 goals in 36 games. In 1961-62 he helped shoot the Reds into Division One with 41 goals at a goal per game as he struck up a prolific partnership with Ian St John, thereby beating Gordon Hodgson's club record set in 1930-31.

In 1965-66, the season of their second title triumph, the Reds didn't lose a First Division game in which Hunt scored. On 6 September 1965 he hit a hat-trick in the space of seven minutes as Liverpool beat West Ham United 5-1. It was certainly no coincidence that Liverpool won the Championship in Hunt's two most prosperous seasons. His emergence as one of the top scorers in the country earned him a place in Alf Ramsey's squad of twenty-two for the 1966 World Cup Finals. Hunt kept Jimmy Greaves out of the line-up and scored three goals, playing in all six games. It was yet another unforgettable season for Hunt - a World Cup winners' medal, a League Championship medal and a European Cup Winners' Cup losers medal. The Anfield fans were not slow to recognise the part Hunt played and soon christened him 'Sir Roger'.

However, although goalscoring was his golden gift, there was more to Roger Hunt. He had an explosive shot and sudden and destructive pace with a phenomenal work-rate. He also possessed neat distribution, good ball control and a good footballing brain. He scored some spectacular goals, including a superb volley that he thrashed into the Inter Milan net during the 1965 European Cup semi-final at Anfield. An even-tempered man, Hunt only once lost his temper - in March 1969 he was substituted in an FA Cup defeat by Leicester City and hurled his shirt into the dugout in frustration!

Earlier that season, Bolton Wanderers had made moves to sign him but Hunt, who'd supported the Trotters as a boy, refused to leave Anfield. However, in December 1969 the Golborne-born striker was persuaded to join the Wanderers in a £32,000 deal. In an eleven season career at Anfield 'Sir Roger' won two League Championship medals, a Second Division medal and an FA Cup winners' medal as well as scoring an astonishing 285 goals in all competitions for Liverpool.

He made his debut for Bolton in a Boxing Day win at Preston but he could do little to revive the Wanderers' fortunes. He did score a hat-trick in a 3-0 win over Birmingham City, though Bolton were relegated to the Third Division for the first time in their history.

In April 1972, over 56,000 attended his testimonial at Anfield to bid farewell to one of Liverpool's favourite sons and all-time great goalscorers.

Honours
League Championship
1963-64, 1965-66,
Second Division Championship
1961-62
FA Cup 1964-65
34 England caps

DAVID JOHNSON

Born	23 October 1951
Birthplace	Liverpool
Height	6ft 0 ins
Weight	12 st 2 lbs

Team	Apps	Gls
Everton	79 (11)	15
Ipswich Town	134 (3)	35
Liverpool	128 (20)	55
Barnsley (L)	4	1
Man City	4 (2)	1
Preston NE	20 (4)	3

One of the few players to have made the short journey both ways across Stanley Park, David Johnson began his Football League career with Everton but despite his early success, which included a hat-trick in an 8-0 win over Southampton, he was transferred to Ipswich town in October 1971. At Portman Road he matured into a useful centre-forward, winning three England caps, the first against Wales in 1975.

In August 1976, Johnson joined Liverpool for a club record £200,000 and was pitched straight into first-team action. Quick, skilful and unselfish, his courageous approach instantly endeared him to the Kop. However, Bob Paisley was blessed with a large and gifted squad and in the course of his permutations over the next two seasons, Johnson was often the man to be left out. Though he wasn't helped by a series of niggling injuries, he managed to collect a League Championship medal and figured in the Wembley defeat by Manchester United but missed out on European glory.

It was hoped that the signing of Kenny Dalglish would give Johnson's career renewed impetus but David Fairclough was often chosen ahead of him to partner the former Celtic star. It wasn't until spring 1978 that Johnson began to look like his old self but with the club's European Cup campaign reaching a climax, he strained knee ligaments and was sidelined for the rest of the season.

Just when it seemed Liverpool were going to discard him, Johnson's luck changed and after two lengthy spells in the side, he struck up an effective partnership with Dalglish that led to more England honours and a few trophies for the Reds. He won a European Cup winners' medal in 1981 plus four League Championship medals. In two campaigns with the Reds, his sharp control, work-rate and ability to take up good positions brought him 37 goals in 63 starts, finishing the 1979-80 season with two goals at Aston Villa to secure a second successive Championship. After that, his scoring rate diminished and, following the emergence of Ian Rush, he found his first team outings were limited.

In August 1982, Johnson's colourful career came full circle when he rejoined Everton for £100,000. Sadly, his second spell with the Blues was nothing short of a disaster; the goal touch, which at one time had made him one of the most feared strikers in Europe, was missing. After a month on loan to Barnsley he moved to Manchester City. He then had a brief spell with Tulsa Roughnecks in the NASL before being transferred to Preston North End where he ended his first-class career.

Nevertheless Johnson remains the only man to score a derby winner for both Everton and Liverpool and occupies a unique place in Merseyside folklore.

Honours
League Championship
1976-77, 1978-79, 1979-80
1981-82
European Cup 1980-81
8 England caps

CRAIG JOHNSTON

Born	8 December 1960
Birthplace	Johannesburg, SA
Height	5ft 8 ins
Weight	10 st 3 lbs

Team	Apps	Gls
Middlesbro'	61 (3)	16
Liverpool	165 (25)	30

South African-born Craig Johnston grew up in Australia where he played for Lake McQuarrie and Sydney City. After seeing Middlesbrough play on tour in New South Wales, he wrote to the club for a trial. He paid his own way to England but Boro manager Jack Charlton decided against keeping the midfield dynamo. However Johnston's persistence paid off when he was offered a second trial by the club's new manager John Neal.

In 1977, he made another mammoth journey from Australia and this time impressed enough to be signed. In the week leading up to his Middlesbrough debut, Johnston was involved in a dramatic sea rescue while swimming in the Channel. But he was fit enough to take the field against Everton in the FA Cup in January 1978. His impressive displays in the Boro midfield soon attracted the attention of international managers and he opted for England over Australia and Scotland for his international hopes and won two Under-21 caps.

In April 1981 Liverpool manager Bob Paisley signed Johnston from Middlesbrough for a fee of £650,000 and immediately dubbed him 'The Headless Chicken' because of his boundless energy and great enthusiasm on the pitch.

Most of Johnston's early appearances for the Reds were as a substitute and it wasn't until March 1982 that he ousted Terry McDermott in the Liverpool side. The Reds then embarked on a surge that was to take them from mid-table to the League Championship.

Although committed in his contribution to the Liverpool team, Johnston did not always conform to the Anfield model and over the club's successful seasons of 1982-83 and 1983-84 he was often at odds with manager Joe Fagan who had replaced Paisley at the helm. Yet it was Fagan who gave Johnston

one of his best runs in the Liverpool team during his seven-year spell at the club. However, after being substituted during the 1984 League Cup Final he walked out of the stadium ignoring the Reds' presentation to the Queen. After this he found himself on the fringe of the action and refused to sign another contract until Fagan had left.

Kenny Dalglish replaced Fagan as Liverpool manager and rebuilt the player's confidence. Johnston became a regular in the side that won the League and FA Cup double in 1985-86. His finest moment in a Liverpool shirt came in the 1986 FA Cup Final when the Reds beat Everton 3-1, the midfielder stabbing home Ian Rush's cross to put them on top.

Over the next couple of seasons Johnston played his best football, his displays being recognised by selection for an England squad. But in May 1988, he announced his retirement and returned to Australia to care for his sister who had been involved in a serious accident and to pursue his other interest, photography.

Johnston later had a spell as a journalist before turning to design and creating the Adidas Predator football boot.

Honours
League Championship
1981-82, 1982-83,
1983-84, 1985-86
FA Cup 1985-86
League Cup
1982-83, 1983-84
European Cup 1983-84

ROB JONES

Born	5 November 1971
Birthplace	Wrexham
Height	5ft 10 ins
Weight	11 st 0 lbs

Team	Apps	Gls
Crewe Alex.	59 (16)	2
Liverpool	182 (1)	0

The grandson of stalwart post-war Liverpool defender Bill Jones, Rob was discovered by Graeme Souness when the Reds' boss was weighing up the merits of another player in the Crewe Alexandra side. When Jones broke into the Railwaymen's side, he was the youngest outfield player the club had ever fielded. A deal was struck in October 1991 with Crewe receiving £300,000 down, £150,000 after the full-back had played 20 games for the Reds and a further £50,000 if he won five England caps.

Though he was clearly an outstanding prospect, Jones' meteoric rise to fame following his move to Anfield was breathtaking. Just two days after putting pen to paper, he was plunged straight into the Liverpool first team, making his debut in a goalless draw against Manchester United in front of an Old Trafford crowd of 44,997. One of the finest young full-backs to emerge since the Second World War, he won his first full cap for England four months later when he played against France. His composed style and mature, level-headed defending impressed all who saw him and he was duly rewarded with an FA Cup winners' medal at the end of the season after helping Liverpool to beat Sunderland.

Jones' affliction with shin splints, an agonising condition which left him barely able to walk after most games, forced him to miss most of the 1992-93 season. Thereafter, despite occasional problems with back and knee and a rather worrying susceptibility to viruses, he began to acquire the top-flight experience he still lacked.

When Roy Evans replaced Graeme Souness as manager, Jones was switched to attacking wing-back, a transition he made with ease. For going forward, he could take part in Liverpool's short passing triangles.

In 1995 he picked up a League Cup winners' medal after the Reds had defeated Bolton Wanderers. Following the arrival of right-sided Jason McAteer from Bolton, Jones

Honours
FA Cup 1991-92
League Cup 1994-95
8 England caps

was switched to the left-back position, playing there in the 1996 FA Cup final defeat by Manchester United. However Jones' back had been causing him great pain and only three days after the match, he was told to rest for six months or risk becoming a cripple.

On his return to the squad, Jones found McAteer and Bjornebye ensconced as wing-backs and so found himself out of the team. Though he began the 1997-98 season extremely well, further injuries meant that he once again experienced mixed fortunes.

On his day, Rob Jones was the complete right-back, decisive in the tackle, winning balls cleanly, passing quickly and accurately over both short and long distances. However, despite pledging his long-term future to the club, Jones missed the entire 1998-99 season through injury and was forced to retire.

Uncertain Beginnings

Very few people outside Merseyside realise that had it not been for a rift in Everton FC in 1892, Liverpool FC would never have existed. A rent dispute at Anfield Road (yes, the very ground that Liverpool use today) caused a core of Everton players and members to look elsewhere for a ground. They chose Goodison Park while the remaining club was forced by the League to change their name from Everton Athletic Grounds Ltd to Liverpool because they did not want two clubs with the name Everton. The rest is, as they say, history!

Here are some more interesting facts about the relationship between the clubs:

* Liverpool still play on Everton's old ground, Anfield. Although the surrounding stands bear no relation to the Anfield that Everton occupied, Liverpool still play on the same pitch. It is still in the same location.

* Everton won their first championship at Anfield.

* Everton hosted an international between England and Ireland at Anfield, it was considered so good at the time.

* The largest audience to ever watch a Derby game at Everton was 78,299 in September 1948 which is also Everton's biggest attendance in history.

KEVIN KEEGAN

Born	14 February 1951
Birthplace	Doncaster
Height	5ft 8 ins
Weight	10 st 10 lbs

Team	Apps	Gls
Scunthorpe U	120 (4)	17
Liverpool	230	68
Southampton	68	37
Newcastle Utd	78	48

When Bill Shankly plucked Kevin Keegan from the obscurity of the lower divisions in 1971, there were few who doubted the wisdom of the Liverpool manager's move. Signed for just £35,000 from Scunthorpe United, Keegan hit Anfield like a tornado. Converted from deep-lying winger to striker, he made his debut for the Reds against Notts County in the opening match of the 1971-72 season and scored after just seven minutes.

Normally, an unknown player like Keegan would have spent an apprenticeship in the reserves but he had the kind of talent that was to turn him into a world-class star. His all-action approach won over the fans and he soon became the idol of the Kop. Bill Shankly called him 'the player who ignited Liverpool' and he certainly was the star of many matches between 1971 and 1977. He was brave, quick and completely inexhaustible. His understanding up front with John Toshack bordered on the telepathic!

Keegan's performance in the 1974 FA Cup Final against Newcastle United, when he scored two goals, was one of his best for the club, although there were the odd turbulent times too in particular the occasion he was sent-off with Leeds' Billy Bremner at Wembley and roughed up by the Belgrade police after walking out on England after being dropped by Don Revie.

The European Cup Final of 1977 against Borussia Moenchengladbach was Keegan's last game in the red of Liverpool. His duel with Bertie Vogts, captain of Borussia and West Germany was a classic - Vogts was reckoned to be the best man-to-man marker in the world but Keegan ran him ragged.

In 1977 he answered the call of continental football and joined SV Hamburg in Germany for £500,000. It made him England's most expensive and best-paid player. During six years at Anfield, he had won three League Championship medals, two UEFA Cup winners' medals and European and FA Cup winners' medals.

Keegan's three years at Hamburg

enhanced his game further, teaching him to overcome man-to-man marking. He had captained England and went on to twice become European Footballer of the Year. He was an excellent finisher with good anticipation and acceleration yet was powerful in the air for someone of his height.

In February 1980, Southampton manager Lawrie McMenemy swooped to sign him and during the 1980-81 season, his 26 goals were sufficient to make Keegan the leading scorer in the First Division, for which he was awarded the Shoot-Adidas Golden Boot.

Keegan made 63 appearances for his country but didn't play for England after the 1982 World Cup, which was a shame for he still had a lot of football in him, as evidenced by a successful two-year spell at Newcastle United during which he led the Magpies back to Division One before deciding to retire.

Keegan had become a folk hero on Tyneside and was welcomed back with open arms when he was appointed Newcastle manager in February 1992. In 1992-93 they won the First Division Championship and were never out of the top six in the Premiership, finishing runners-up on two occasions. Following his sudden resignation, Keegan then took charge at Fulham, later becoming England's caretaker-manager. After taking the Cottagers to the Second Division Championship, he took on the poisoned chalice of the England job full-time but resigned after a home defeat by Germany and a disappointing European Championships. He is now back in club management with newly-promoted Manchester City.

Honours
League Championship
1972-73, 1975-76, 1976-77
FA Cup 1973-74
European Cup 1976-77
UEFA Cup 1972-73, 1975-76
63 England caps

ALAN KENNEDY

Born	31 August 1954
Birthplace	Sunderland
Height	5ft 9 ins
Weight	10 st 7 lbs

Team	Apps	Gls
Newcastle U	155 (3)	9
Liverpool	249 (2)	15
Sunderland	54	2
Hartlepool U	4 (1)	0
Wigan Ath.	22	0
Wrexham	15 (1)	0

On beginning his career with Newcastle United, Alan Kennedy rapidly became a terrace favourite once he had tasted first-team action as a teenager. Brave and tough in the tackle, he had the crowd roaring in anticipation. After only a handful of senior outings, he appeared for the Magpies in the 1974 FA Cup Final against Liverpool that the Reds won 3-0. With United he was capped at Under-23 and 'B' level and was also selected for a full England place in 1975 but a knee injury prevented his appearance. He didn't get another chance to play for his country for almost a decade but by that time he had joined Liverpool, leaving St James' Park after the Magpies' relegation in 1978. The fee of £300,000 was considered a massive outlay for a full-back but it was believed that Kennedy was approaching his prime and would benefit from playing alongside top performers week in, week out.

The Kop nicknamed him 'Barney Rubble' after the Flintstones cartoon character and although he started in the Reds' side as an out-and-out winger, Kennedy switched to defence and never looked back, helping the club win the League Championship in his first two seasons at Anfield.

When his character was put to the test in 1980-81, Kennedy was not found wanting. Though he struck an inconsistent patch of form and lost his place in the side, he fought back to regain his place in time for the European Cup Final against Real Madrid in Paris. In the 84th minute of the most memorable game of Kennedy's Liverpool career, with the score level at 0-0, he made a sudden darting run into the box and smashed the ball past the perplexed keeper Agustin.

Despite coming under pressure on the

arrival of Mark Lawrenson, Kennedy again re-established himself in the Liverpool team and helped the Reds win three more consecutive League Championship titles, being an ever-present in 1982-83 and 1983-84. During the 1984 European Cup Final, he secured the treble for Liverpool, scoring the deciding penalty in a shoot-out with Roma in Rome. The capture of the European Cup, League Championship and League Cup led to Kennedy being selected for England by Bobby Robson later that summer. In 1985 however, he was replaced in the Liverpool side by Jim Beglin and joined his home-town club Sunderland for £100,000. He had won every major honour except the FA Cup more than once and his contribution to Liverpool's success should not be overlooked.

After a spell playing for Hartlepool United and abroad with Beerschot of Belgium, Kennedy joined Wigan Athletic. He then played non-League football for Colne Dynamoes before returning to league action with Wrexham. Another spell of non-League football with Morecambe followed before he became player-manager of Netherfield. After ending his career with Barrow, Alan Kennedy became a radio presenter on Merseyside as well as an accomplished after-dinner speaker.

Honours
League Championship
1978-79, 1979-80, 1981-82, 1982-83, 1983-84
League Cup 1980-81, 1981-82, 1982-83, 1983-84
European Cup
1980-81, 1983-84
2 England caps

RAY KENNEDY

Born	28 July 1951
Birthplace	Seaton Delaval
Height	5ft 11 ins
Weight	13 st 0 lbs

Team	Apps	Gls
Arsenal	156 (2)	53
Liverpool	272 (3)	51
Swansea C	42	2
Hartlepool U	18 (5)	3

Ray Kennedy joined Arsenal as an apprentice in April 1968 after having been rejected by Port Vale and going to work in a sweet factory. Little did he realise at that time but he was to become the most honoured player (in terms of medals won) in the history of English football. After two seasons in the Gunners' reserve side, he made his League debut against Sunderland in February 1970. He shot to fame after scoring one of Arsenal's goals in that season's two-legged Inter Cities Fairs Cup Final as the Gunners beat Anderlecht 4-3 on aggregate. He became a regular in the Arsenal side the following season, ending the campaign in which the club did the double with 26 goals as well as being selected for England's Under-23 side and winning Rothman's Young Player of the Year award. He spent a further three seasons at Highbury, winning another FA Cup winners' medal in 1971-72 and six Under-23 caps.

Kennedy arrived at Anfield as Bill Shankly's last signing at the club, although injury kept him out of the first four games of the 1974-75 season. Impressing new manager Bob Paisley, he ousted Welsh international John Toshack from the starting line-up, scoring 10 goals in 24 games before the former Cardiff striker was recalled in a bid to find a winning blend. However, towards the end of the campaign, Paisley began to experiment, playing Kennedy in a deep-lying position behind the twin strike force of Keegan and Toshack. By November 1975, Kennedy was installed on the left side of Liverpool's midfield and over the next six years or so helped the Reds win ten major honours.

scored some vital goals for the Reds, including a late strike against Bayern Munich in the 1981 European Cup semi-final and a second-half volley against Bruges when the Belgians were 2-0 up in the 1976 UEFA Cup Final. Ultimately squeezed out of the Liverpool side by Ronnie Whelan, the England international joined Swansea City for a fee of £160,000.

He made his Swans debut against Manchester United, his presence in midfield being instrumental in the Welsh club winning 2-0 as he set up goals for Alan Curtis and Leighton James. The Swans were unbeaten in Kennedy's first nine games for the club but the following season he returned to his native north-east to play for Hartlepool United.

After a spell as a publican and a coaching appointment at Sunderland, it was revealed that Ray Kennedy was suffering from Parkinson's Disease. Since then he has spent his time raising public awareness of the illness and dealing with his own health and personal problems. In 1991, a special match was staged between Liverpool and Arsenal to finance the former Red's medical treatment.

Though he was short of pace, Kennedy read the game well and could change the emphasis of a game with a sweeping crossfield pass, though his deadliest attribute was the ability to make a late run into the box to finish off a move at the far post. He

Honours
League Championship
1975-76, 1976-77, 1978-79, 1979-80, 1981-82
League Cup 1980-81
European Cup
1976-77, 1977-78
17 England caps

CHRIS LAWLER

Born	20 October 1943
Birthplace	Liverpool
Height	6ft 0 ins
Weight	12 st 10 lbs

Team	Apps	Gls
Liverpool	406	41
Portsmouth	35 (1)	0
Stockport Co.	33 (3)	3

Chris Lawler, the man they called 'The Silent Knight', scored 61 goals for Liverpool in a playing career that spanned more than 14 years. The full-back made his Reds' debut in March 1963 against West Bromwich Albion at Anfield in a 2-2 draw. His first goal for the club came in a 5-1 demolition of Burnley at Turf Moor in 1964. His ability to pop up in the opposition's penalty area and tuck the ball away made him one of the greatest full-backs in Liverpool's history. He became a regular choice in the Liverpool side in 1964-65 when he completed a successful season by winning an FA Cup winners' medal as the Reds beat Leeds United 2-1 after extra-time.

Lawler was incredibly loyal to Liverpool and even postponed his wedding when the Reds played Inter Milan in the 1965 European Cup semi-final. A remarkable statistic concerning Chris Lawler was his 11 goals in 66 appearances in European football. One of the full-back's most inspired performances came against Honved of Hungary in the 1965-66 European Cup Winners' Cup. After a goalless draw in Hungary, the Reds went all out for an early goal in the return leg at Anfield. Lawler struck with a header after Peter Thompson had hit a post and then the full-back saw two great attempts strike the woodwork and narrowly miss with two others. That season, Lawler missed just two games through injury as Liverpool won the League Championship - one of his five goals coming after just 20 seconds in the 2-2 draw with Sunderland at Roker Park.

Lawler was chosen to play for

England and made his international debut four days after appearing in the FA Cup Final against Arsenal in May 1971, against Malta in a European Championship qualifier. He scored in a 5-0 Wembley victory and went on to win three more caps, never playing on the losing side.

Lawler was an ever-present in 1971-72 and again the following season when Liverpool won both the League Championship and the UEFA Cup. Sadly a knee injury sustained at Loftus Road ended his proud record of consistency and despite a handful of appearances, he was never the same again.

After a move to Manchester City was called off by Liverpool at the last minute, Lawler was transferred to Portsmouth in October 1975, where he joined up with former team-mate Ian St John, by then Pompey manager. Though he failed to score, he made 36 appearances for the south coast club before joining Stockport County in the summer of 1977. In the twilight of his career he managed another 36 appearances and scored three goals.

On hanging up his boots, Lawler ended up back at Anfield and was a member of the famous bootroom, coaching the club's youngsters. However, during the reign of Kenny Dalglish, Lawler left the club he had served so well as a magnificent full-back and goalscorer. His coolness, control and attacking skills will live long in the memories of Liverpool supporters.

Honours
League Championship
1965-66, 1972-73
FA Cup 1964-65
UEFA Cup 1972-73
4 England caps

TOMMY LAWRENCE

Born	14 May 1940
Birthplace	Dailly
Height	5ft 11 ins
Weight	13 st 12 lbs

Team	Apps	Gls
Liverpool	306	0
Tranmere R	80	0

When Bill Shankly arrived at Anfield in the summer of 1959, he found Tommy Lawrence lingering in Liverpool's reserve side, having served a two-year apprenticeship in the club's Central League team. When the club's regular 'keeper Jim Furnell damaged a finger, Shankly promoted Lawrence and he became impossible to displace thereafter. Affectionately known as 'The Flying Pig' Lawrence was never a spectacular goalkeeper but was always very dependable. What the Scottish keeper lacked in height he made up for with his acute positional sense, while he possessed an athleticism that belied is bulk. Defenders liked him; they knew where they were with him and could trust in his reliability.

Lawrence operated behind a Liverpool back four that usually played square and that pushed upfield whenever possible. Ever alert, Lawrence would race from his area to clear the impending danger should the Reds' defence be breached by an opponent's run from midfield or a penetrating pass. However, Liverpool's defence was so good that Lawrence's problem was often maintaining concentration. He had to laugh when Bill Shankly outlined his dream: 'Wouldn't it be great if we could put a deckchair in the middle of the goal, you sitting in it, cigar in your mouth. When the ball comes, you get out, catch it and say 'It's a lovely day to play football isn't it?' It has to be said that Shankly uttered these words after Liverpool had won the title and still had a couple of meaningless games to play!

point in a 5-0 demolition of Arsenal that clinched the title. His consistency in the Liverpool goal over the next few seasons was remarkable, it being a complete mystery that his international recall should have been delayed for six years. Even then it was limited to two matches, in both of which he found himself unfairly blamed for some of the goals.

Lawrence and his defence conceded just 24 goals in 1968-69, thereby establishing a new Football League record. He remained Liverpool's first-choice goalkeeper until February 1970 when an injury gave understudy Ray Clemence a chance to stake his claim and in the face of competition from the future England international, Lawrence moved across the Mersey to play for Tranmere Rovers.

After two-and-a-half seasons as the Prenton Park Club's first-choice keeper, Lawrence, whose heart belonged to Anfield, left to play non-League football for Chorley. He now works night shifts at a wire factory in Warrington.

After just one season in the Liverpool side, Lawrence won the first of three full caps for Scotland when he played in a 1-0 defeat at the hands of the Republic of Ireland. The following season - 1963-64 - brought a League Championship medal and Lawrence climaxed an accomplished campaign by brilliantly saving a George Eastham penalty, the turning

Honours
**League Championship
1963-64, 1965-66
FA Cup 1964-65
3 England caps**

MARK LAWRENSON

Born	2 June 1957
Birthplace	Preston
Height	6ft 0 ins
Weight	11 st 7 lbs

Team	Apps	Gls
Preston NE	73 (2)	2
Brighton & HA	152	5
Liverpool	233 (8)	11

Mark Lawrenson was without doubt one of the most stylish and polished defenders of the modern era, winning almost every honour in the game with Liverpool in the 1980s. Born just a stone's throw away from Preston North End's Deepdale ground, he followed in his father Tommy's footsteps by joining the Lilywhites, having rejected the opportunity to pursue a cricketing career with Lancashire. He signed professional forms for North End in August 1974 and after some impressive displays in the club's Central League side, he made his Football League debut in a 2-2 draw against Watford towards the end of the 1974-75 season.

At Deepdale a chance conversation with former Preston favourite Alan Kelly, who was then coach to both North End and the Republic of Ireland, led to Lawrenson, whose mother was born in Waterford, playing for the Irish.

He won the first of 39 caps against Poland in April 1977, but three months later was on his way to Brighton and Hove Albion for £100,000 (Liverpool reportedly just failed with a £70,000 bid for the player). He didn't want to leave Deepdale but North End needed the money and so cashed in their most valuable asset. At the time the deal went through, he was on holiday and agreed the transfer in a café on the sea front in Benidorm! He spent four years on the south coast, helping the Seagulls win promotion to the First Division in 1978-79 and played a total of 152 league games for the team, before Liverpool paid a record-breaking £900,000 for his services in August 1981.

With Phil Neal, Alan Hansen and Steve Nicol alongside him, Lawrenson reached the pinnacle of his career with the Reds. He remained a regular in the side in various positions throughout the decade and in doing so picked up

his last season at Anfield in 1987-88.

At international level Lawrenson scored five goals, including a couple in the record 8-0 home victory over Malta in November 1983 but his most memorable contribution was the goal that beat Scotland at Hampden Park in February 1987 and sent the Republic on their way to the 1988 European Championships in Germany while he also captained the Irish on his final international appearance, leading them to a 5-0 victory over Israel.

In April 1988 he took up the offer of a managerial post with Oxford United. After some success he was sacked after a disagreement with the club's directors over the sale of Dean Saunders to Derby County. After a brief spell as player-coach at Tampa Bay Rowdies, he became manager of Peterborough United but after spells in charge of a number of non-League clubs, he is now a prominent television and radio personality.

League Championship and League Cup winners' medals in successive seasons in 1981-82, 1982-83 and 1983-84. He won a European Cup winners' medal in 1984 and a runners-up medal in the same competition the following year after the ill-fated clash with Juventus at the Heysel Stadium. Lawrenson was a double winner in 1985-86 when Liverpool won both the League and the FA Cup. Another League Championship medal was added to the collection in

Honours
League Championship
1981-82, 1982-83, 1983-84
1985-86, 1987-88
FA Cup 1985-86
League Cup
1981-82, 1982-83, 1983-84
European Cup 1983-84
39 Republic of Ireland caps

SAMMY LEE

Born	7 February 1959
Birthplace	Liverpool
Height	5ft 5 ins
Weight	10 st 1 lbs

Team	Apps	Gls
Liverpool	190 (7)	13
Q.P.R.	29 (1)	0
Southampton	0 (2)	0
Bolton W	4	0

Scouser Sammy Lee made his League debut as a substitute against Leicester City at Anfield in April 1978, scoring in a 3-2 victory but was then stranded on the fringe of the side for the next two years. At 5ft 5ins and weighing just over 10 stones, he did not at first appear to have the build of a footballer but that was deceptive; he was as fast, resilient and determined as any man on the pitch. He was a driving force, urging the team forward all the time with his boyish enthusiasm but just as ready to sprint back into defence.

It was midway through the 1980-81 season when Sammy Lee displaced Jimmy Case on the right side of the Reds' midfield. He quickly endeared himself to the Liverpool fans with his 'never-say-die' approach and became a fixture in the Reds' side that won three successive League Championships, two European Cups and four League Cups. Lee's play was reminiscent of Ian Callaghan and though he lacked the great Anfield clubman's pace, his tackling was more fierce and he provided cover when full-back Phil Neal ventured forward. Perhaps his most valuable defensive display came in the 1984 European Cup Final against AS Roma as the Reds were forced to withstand periods of heavy pressure before going on to win on penalties.

Though his strike-rate for Liverpool was disappointing, Lee scored from a powerfully hit free-kick on his full international debut for England against Greece. Finding the net had never been Sammy Lee's priority and at the start of the 1984-85 season he seemed set for many more campaigns at the top - he was only 25, at the peak of his powers and an established

England international. However, fitness problems and a loss off form sadly conspired to shatter the midfielder's confidence and with the likes of Craig Johnston and Steve Nicol appearing on the scene, he gradually faded out of contention.

In August 1986, Lee left his beloved Anfield for Queen's Park Rangers but he failed to settle at Loftus Road and a year later, he went to Spain to play for Osasuna. He performed creditably in the Spanish League but in January 1990 he returned to England and signed an 18-month contract with Southampton.

At the Dell, Lee linked up with Jimmy Case but injuries prevented him from making much of an impression and in October 1990 he was signed by another of his former Anfield teammates, Bolton Wanderers' manager Phil Neal. Brought to Burnden Park to bolster the club's promotion push, he again suffered from injuries and managed only five first team appearances and though he returned to full fitness early in 1991-92, he failed to regain selection for the Wanderers' first team.

In the summer of 1992, Lee returned to his roots, joining Liverpool on the coaching staff and later becoming the club's reserve team and fitness coach, a position which he now also holds with the senior England team.

Honours
League Championship
1981-82, 1982-83, 1983-84, 1985-86
League Cup 1980-81,
1981-82, 1982-83, 1983-84
European Cup
1980-81, 1983-84
14 England caps

BILLY LIDDELL

Born	10 January 1922
Birthplace	Dunfermline
Height	5ft 10 ins
Weight	12 st 11 lbs

Team	Apps	Gls
Liverpool	495	216

Billy Liddell joined Liverpool as an 18-year-old from the Fifeshire junior club, Lochgelly Violet and began to learn his trade in the Lancashire midweek League, only to see the first six years of his career lost to the war. Though he served as an RAF navigator, he played almost 150 games for the Reds as football continued on a regional basis, netting a hat-trick in a 7-3 win over Manchester City. His reputation as a flying winger with a powerful shot in either foot was growing as he made eight appearances for Scotland in wartime internationals.

Liddell didn't make his official Liverpool debut until January 1946 when, five days short of his 24th birthday, he scored in an FA Cup third round tie against Chester.

In 1946-47 he played in 35 games as Liverpool won the first post-war League Championship. Revealing the pace and power that were to be his hallmarks for almost fifteen years, Liddell also showed the dashing style that was to make him one of Liverpool's most prolific goalscorers.

In 1949-50, Liverpool were unbeaten in their opening nineteen matches, setting a record in a 42-match season. During that run, Liddell was at his best, creating havoc among opposition defences and scoring goals. Unfortunately, he didn't add an FA Cup winners' medal to it, for Arsenal beat the Reds 2-0 in the final. A vital member of the Scottish national side, he and Stanley Matthews were the two players to appear in both the Great Britain v Rest of the World and Rest of Europe matches.

"In 1946-47 he was a major factor in Liverpool's first post-war League Championship - revealing the pace and power that were to be his hallmarks for almost fifteen years,."

When Liverpool were relegated to the Second Division at the end of the 1952-53 season, Liddell's reaction was typical of the man. He showed great determination and in his first four seasons out of the top flight, he scored 101 goals in 156 League games. He could torture defences - take your eyes off him for a moment and the chances were that you would pay with a goal. He was so popular and had such an immense influence on the side that the fans re-christened the club 'Liddellpool' and made Billy Liddell their 'King'.

During Billy Liddell's last season, the attendances at Anfield started to drop. Almost 44,000 had watched the opening match but only 13,000 watched the final home game. Yet the loyalty of the fans towards Billy Liddell remained unchanged: over 38,000 paid tribute to him in a benefit match between Liverpool and an All-Star team.

One of the greatest Anfield heroes of all-time, Billy Liddell set a wonderful example to any young player aspiring to greatness and on his retirement he became a bursar at Liverpool University after studying accountancy throughout his playing career. He was also appointed a Justice of the Peace and undertook a great amount of work for boys' clubs.

Honours
League Championship
1946-47
28 Scotland caps

ALEC LINDSAY

Born	27 February 1948
Birthplace	Bury
Height	5ft 9 ins
Weight	11 st 0 lbs

Team	Apps	Gls
Bury	126	14
Liverpool	168 (2)	12
Stoke City	20	3

Alec Lindsay began his Football League career with his home-town club Bury, joining the Gigg Lane club as an apprentice in March 1965. A former England youth international, he helped the Shakers win promotion to the Second Division in 1967-68 before joining Liverpool for a fee of £67,000 in March 1969. The club had watched him on a number of occasions but were never sure as to his best position. Indeed, he was used at Bury as a wing-half, inside-forward and even on the wing in a couple of games.

Like so many newcomers to Anfield from the lower divisions, Lindsay went straight into the club's Central League side. After taking longer than most to settle with the Reds, he made his debut and several further unremarkable appearances in midfield before being

switched to the left-back berth he was to grace so stylishly.

During Lindsay's early days at Anfield, Bill Shankly advised him that he was less than satisfied with his performances to date and reminded him that when he had been at Bury, he had left defenders in his wake with his speed and skill, to which the Reds' defender replied 'but boss that was not me.' A bemused Shankly turned to Bob Paisley and said 'By Christ Bob, we've signed the wrong man!'

The left-back position at Anfield had been a problem area following the premature retirement through injury of Gerry Byrne. A number of payers had been tried before Lindsay was given his chance. He took to the role like a duck to water and made the position his own. With Chris Lawler at right-back and Lindsay on the left, the Reds' defence always opted for playing itself out of trouble. Lawler and Lindsay always wanted to play football and they would initiate and control many a Liverpool attack.

The highlights of Alec Lindsay's stay at Anfield were a UEFA Cup winners' medal in 1973, a League Championship medal in the same year and an FA Cup winners' medal in 1974. In the final against Newcastle United, he was in tremendous form. Prominent on the overlap, he drove a ferocious cross-shot past keeper Ian McFaul only to have his joy cut short by an offside whistle. He was probably at the peak of his form in 1974 when he was capped four times by England when Joe Mercer was caretaker manager, the first in a 2-2 draw with Argentina.

Unfortunately, Lindsay's form deteriorated shortly afterwards mainly because of personal problems and he was never the same player again. He signed for Stoke City in August 1977 but played only 20 games, scoring three goals before trying his luck in the United States and Canada. His last club was Toronto Blizzards in 1979 before he turned his back on football for good.

For such a talented footballer, it is a tragedy that Lindsay's career ended at the age of 31, although to be fair, it was really over when he left Anfield two years earlier.

Honours
League Championship
1972-73
FA Cup 1973-74
UEFA Cup 1972-73
4 England caps

TERRY McDERMOTT

Born	8 December 1951
Birthplace	Kirkby
Height	5ft 9 ins
Weight	12 st 13 lbs

Team	Apps	Gls
Bury	83 (7)	8
Newcastle Utd	129 (1)	18
Liverpool	221 (11)	54

Though Liverpool born, Terry McDermott began his footballing career with homely Bury before his transfer to Newcastle United in January 1973. Although on the losing side in the 1974 FA Cup Final against Liverpool, McDermott had been particularly impressive for the Magpies. A clash with Newcastle boss Joe Harvey led to his transfer to Liverpool for a fee of £170,000.

McDermott went straight into the Liverpool side but failed to settle as the Reds' new manager Bob Paisley experimented in an attempt to continue where Bill Shankly had left off. Liverpool won the League Championship and UEFA Cup in 1975-76 without McDermott's assistance and it seemed only a matter of time before his arrival would be written off as an expensive mistake and he would be transferred. However, Bob Paisley kept faith with him and the following season saw him firmly established by the spring, playing a memorable role in the run-in which saw the League title and the European Cup come to Anfield but the FA Cup go to Old Trafford.

"McDermott was dangerous when running from deep positions and arriving late in the penalty area, where his finishing could be deadly."

McDermott was superb and dangerous when running from deep positions and arriving late in the penalty area, where his finishing could be deadly. The 1976-77 campaign saw him score two really outstanding goals. The first came at Maine Road in the FA Cup semi-final against Everton as he spotted goalkeeper David Lawson off his line and chipped in a beautiful goal. The second was probably the most important goal of his career. It broke the deadlock in the 1977 European Cup Final against Borussia

Moenchengladbach in Rome. He ghosted down the inside-right channel to receive Steve Heighway's pass and curl the ball in superb fashion round the German keeper.

The following year, when Graeme Souness arrived at Anfield, McDermott reached his peak. The Scot's style of play allowed the wiry McDermott the freedom he needed to express his talents fully. He covered every inch of he grass on the pitch, often acting as a decoy and creating space for his colleagues to exploit. When in possession, his control and instinctive passing ability allowed him to get the best out of the situation.

In September 1978 McDermott started and finished one of Anfield's best-ever goals in the televised 7-0 hammering of Spurs. In 1979-80 he was the Reds' top scorer with 13 goals, netting a hat-trick against Oulu Palloseura the Finnish champions in a 10-1 victory.

In 1980 he became the first man to win awards from the Football Writers' Association and his fellow players in the same season.

McDermott made another valuable contribution in 1981-82, getting 14 goals in 28 games as Liverpool won the League

title and Milk Cup. Then he seemed to lose a little impetus and he returned to the north-east to team up with Kevin Keegan at Newcastle, helping the club return to the top flight. He later played for Cork City and Apoel of Cyprus before returning to Newcastle for a third time as Keegan's right-hand man where he became a success in management too.

Honours
League Championship
1976-77, 1978-79, 1979-80, 1981-82
League Cup
1980-81, 1981-82
European Cup
1976-77, 1977-78, 1980-81
25 England caps

STEVE McMAHON

Born	20 August 1961
Birthplace	Liverpool
Height	5ft 9 ins
Weight	11 st 8 lbs

Team	Apps	Gls
Everton	99 (1)	11
Aston Villa	74 (1)	7
Liverpool	202 (2)	29
Man City	83 (4)	1
Swindon Town	38 (4)	0

A former Goodison ball boy, Steve McMahon joined Everton as an apprentice and, after working his way up through the ranks, made his Football League debut at Sunderland in August 1980. The following season he was voted the Blues' Player of the Year by supporters who appreciated his honest endeavour and total commitment. A bright future certainly seemed assured when he was selected to play for the England Under-21 side against the Republic of Ireland.

McMahon continued to perform at a consistently high level though he was not playing in a particularly good Everton side. Eventually the midfielder came to the conclusion that the only way to further his career was to leave Goodison. His contract expired at the end of the 1982-83 season and he refused to sign another even though new manager Howard Kendall was adamant that he wanted McMahon to stay. Liverpool made a firm offer for him but after discussions with his family, he opted to join Aston Villa for £250,000. However, he failed to settle in the Midlands and in September 1985 he became Kenny Dalglish's first signing when he moved to Anfield for £350,000.

McMahon was bought to fulfil a very specific brief. Dalglish realised the departure of Graeme Souness had left a chasm in the Reds' midfield, a gap that had never been properly filled until McMahon. His abrasive ball-winning qualities, fine distribution and dynamic shooting were soon in evidence. Ironically, his first goal for the Reds was the winner at Goodison in the Merseyside derby. In that first season as a Red, McMahon won a League Championship medal but vied for a place with Kevin MacDonald and missed the FA Cup Final victory over Everton.

The following campaign saw a maturing of his talents but it was not until 1987-88 and the arrival of John

Barnes and Peter Beardsley that McMahon began to realise his full potential. Strong, hard tackling remained a basic part of his game but he now revealed creativity and vision. Both his long and short passing grew in control and penetration and though never a prolific scorer, he continued to contribute a number of spectacular goals.

McMahon's success at Liverpool also brought him England honours with 17 caps including a place in Bobby Robson's 1990 World Cup squad. He also picked up further League Championship medal and FA Cup honours at Anfield. The great irony of his Liverpool career is the fact that it was curtailed by the very man he was bought to replace, Graeme Souness. After six seasons at the club, McMahon was transferred to Manchester City for £900,000, joining former Everton team-mate Peter Reid, who was then the Maine Road club's boss.

In November 1994 he was appointed player-manager of Swindon Town and though the club suffered successive relegations, McMahon inspired the Robins to win the Second Division Championship in 1995-96, his first full season at the County Ground.

Later relieved of his duties, McMahon is now manager of Blackpool, who helped to promotion to the Second Division via the play-offs in 2000-01.

Honours
League Championship
1985-86, 1987-88, 1989-90
FA Cup
1988-89
17 England caps

STEVE McMANAMAN

Born	11 February 1972
Birthplace	Liverpool
Height	6ft 0 ins
Weight	10 st 6 lbs

Team	Apps	Gls
Liverpool	258 (14)	46

Steve McManaman was the first product of Liverpool's modern youth system to break through into the big time. By the age of twenty-three he was a full England international and had both winners' medals and 'man-of-the-Match' awards from FA and League Cup Finals.

McManaman was thrown into the Liverpool side as a right-winger midway through the 1990-91 season as a clearly gifted but distinctly frail-looking 18-year-old. He immediately impressed with his speed, skill and trickery and made a telling contribution to the 1992 FA Cup triumph against Sunderland. Ideally, he might have been blooded rather more gradually than the club's prevailing injury situation permitted and over the next couple of seasons he did not progress as rapidly as expected. However, when he was handed a free role in Roy Evans' new-look formation of 1994-95, he quickly matured into the most dangerous attacker in English football with intelligence, awareness and tactical appreciation.

Though his goalscoring record was not as healthy as it might have been, it didn't prevent McManaman from producing the occasional sensational strike. His brace against Bolton Wanderers in the 1995 Coca Cola Cup Final were among the finest goals ever seen at Wembley. In 1995-96 he enjoyed one of his best seasons for Liverpool as an ever-present and established himself as a regular choice for the England team. He had an excellent Euro '96, the home nation being unlucky to lose out to the Germans at the semi-final sage.

The only thing that appeared to pose any sort of threat to his continued rise was the demand placed on McManaman's talents by both club and country, this being borne out by days of sheer brilliance and those where little went right. However, at his peak his maze-like runs found their way through tight-packed defences to help unlock games that appeared to be going nowhere and it was on these occasions that the big foreign clubs cast envious eyes in his direction.

McManaman continued to score some brilliant individual goals during 1997-98, in particular the goal against Celtic at Parkhead in the UEFA Cup having all the hallmarks of this lively and dangerous old-fashioned winger. Unbelievably, he was called upon just once during World Cup '98 in France when he came on for the last quarter-of-an-hour of the first round with the instruction to run at the Colombian defence.

During the course of the 1998-99 season, there was much transfer speculation and this inevitably upset the Reds' performances. Eventually got an offer he couldn't refuse and joined Real Madrid in July 1999.

Though some Liverpool supporters would argue that for too long the Reds built the side around him, there is no doubt that McManaman was a good servant to the Anfield club. His ability to beat player after player and find the net was a welcome breath of fresh air in a Liverpool side often bereft of

such skill during the 1990s.

On 24 May 2000 McManaman scored the goal of his life and a place in history, helping Real Madrid capture the European Cup for the eighth time, beating Valencia 3-0. The former Reds' winger's 67th minute volley made him the first Englishman to score for a foreign side in a European final. He repeated the feat last season, appearing in Real's triumph against Bayer Leverkusen at Hampden Park.

Honours
FA Cup 1991-92
League Cup 1994-95
37 England caps

JIMMY MELIA

Born	1 November 1937
Birthplace	Liverpool
Height	5ft 9ins
Weight	10st 12lbs

Team	Apps	Gls
Liverpool	269	76
Wolves	24	4
Southampton	139	11
Aldershot	135	14
Crewe Alex.	2 (2)	0

One of the most constructive players Liverpool have ever had, Jimmy Melia celebrated his Football League debut in December 1955 with a goal against Nottingham Forest. By midway through the following season, he had established himself as a regular member of a Liverpool side constantly pushing for promotion to the top flight.

Melia's most successful season in terms of goals scored was 1958-59 when he netted 21 times. A master of the penetrating through pass and adept at shielding the ball, he did occasionally over-elaborate when in possession, which along with an odd tendency to drift in and out of a game, infuriated Koppites. Their abuse was particularly scathing when Melia missed a penalty five minutes from time in an important promotion battle against Brighton and Hove Albion with the Seagulls leading 1-0. However, demonstrating his usual resilience, he had the great satisfaction of heading the Reds' equaliser in the dying moments of the game.

Melia saved his most impressive form for the club's Second Division Championship winning season of 1961-62 when the Reds finished eight points clear of runners-up Leyton Orient.

As far as international honours were concerned, Jimmy Melia remained in the shadow of Johnny Haynes and had to wait until the Fulham inside-forward was involved in a car crash before breaking into the England side against Scotland. He gained a second cap as England beat Switzerland 8-1 in Basle with Melia scoring one of his side's goals.

Back at Anfield, Melia's subtle promptings helped the Reds into a Championship challenging position but shortly before Christmas 1963, a minor ankle injury sidelined the prematurely balding schemer. Liverpool manager Bill Shankly was forced to make a change to his normally reliable line-up and because there was no obvious ready-made replacement for Melia, he switched Ian St John to a deep-lying position to take some of the midfield responsibility and promoted Alf Arrowsmith from the Central League side to partner Roger Hunt up front. Though he made a brief reappearance later in the season, a campaign in which the Reds won the League Championship, Melia's Anfield days were over and in March 1964 he was transferred to Wolverhampton Wanderers for £55,000.

His stint at Molineux was not a successful one and he moved on to Southampton, who paid a club record £30,000 for his services. After helping the Saints win promotion to the First Division, Melia joined Aldershot as player-manager. He was a flamboyant manager, leading the Shots to the fourth round of the FA Cup in 1969-70. However, midway through the 1971-72 season with Aldershot in a lowly position, he was sacked. He took over a similar post with Crewe

Alexandra but the Railwaymen had to seek re-election twice with Melia in charge.

Melia lasted three months at Southport and nine months at Brighton, who also reached the FA Cup Final in his spell there. He later worked in Portugal and was in charge of Stockport County before going to coach in the United States.

Honours
League Championship
1963-64
Second Division Championship
1961-62
2 England caps

GORDON MILNE

Born	29 March 1937	
Birthplace	Preston	
Height	5ft 8ins	
Weight	11st 3lbs	

Team	Apps	Gls
Preston NE	81	3
Liverpool	234 (2)	18
Blackpool	60 (4)	4

Bill Shankly had known Gordon Milne since the latter was a toddler, having played with his father Jimmy during their days at Preston North End. So it was hardly surprising that Shankly knew what he was buying when he paid North End £316,000 for Milne's services in the summer of 1960.

However, Milne made an indifferent start with his new club. After being preferred to the experienced Johnny Wheeler, he lost his place to the veteran wing-half who was enjoying an Indian summer. He fought back to regain his place and soon became a permanent fixture in the Liverpool midfield. A key member of the Reds' Second Division Championship winning side, he was the first Shankly signing destined to play a role in Liverpool's success of the 1960s.

Milne picked up a League Championship winners' medal in 1963-64 but was forced to miss the 1965 FA Cup Final victory over Leeds United after an injury sustained in a 4-0 Good Friday defeat by Chelsea at Stamford Bridge. The following season he was back to his best, helping the Reds to yet another League Championship success and playing in the European Cup Winners' Cup Final against Borussia Dortmund at Hampden Park, which Liverpool lost 2-1.

Though he was capped 14 times by England at full international level, Milne did not feature in Alf Ramsey's World Cup team.

A stocky and industrious wing-half, Milne relied on anticipation to make interceptions before setting up attacks with precise distribution. Though he often popped up around the opposition's penalty area, he failed to find the back of the net on a regular basis. Yet during the course of the club's League Championship success of 1965-66 he netted vital winners in the defeats over fellow contenders Burnley (home 2-1), Leeds United (away 1-0) and Manchester United (home 2-1).

In May 1967, Milne, who many supporters thought still had plenty to offer, left Anfield to move up the coast to play for Blackpool, for £30,000. Following his brief sojourn at Bloomfield Road, Milne became player-manager of Wigan Athletic, who in 1970-71 won the Northern Premier League title and had a good run in the FA Cup. After a spell as England youth team manager, he took charge of Coventry City. At Highfield Road, Milne produced some fine players through the youth scheme but his sides never seemed to fulfil their potential and the Sky Blues' directors and fans eventually lost patience with him.

On becoming manager of Leicester City, he led the Foxes into the First Division after a late run saw them squeeze home. Some two months after his contract with City expired in May 1987, he accepted an offer to manage Turkish club Besiktas. Under Milne's leadership they won the Turkish Cup in 1989, did the double in 1990 and took further League Championships in 1991 and 1992 when they remained unbeaten all term. Milne then managed Nagoya Grampus Eight of Japan before departing at the same time as Gary Lineker. Later he was appointed Chief Executive of the League Managers' Association.

Honours
League Championship
1963-64, 1965-66
Second Division Championship
1961-62
14 England caps

JAN MOLBY

Born	1 July 1963
Birthplace	Kolding, Denmark
Height	6ft 1ins
Weight	14st 7lbs

Team	Apps	Gls
Liverpool	195 (23)	44
Barnsley (L)	5	0
Norwich C (L)	3	0
Swansea City	39 (2)	8

Jan Molby joined Liverpool in the summer of 1984 following a successful stay with the Dutch side Ajax of Amsterdam. The £575,000 signing made his League debut at Norwich City in August 1984, his great influence in midfield minimising the loss of Graeme Souness to Italian football, although later Kenny Dalglish used him as a 'sweeper'. In 1985-86, Molby played in 39 League games as Liverpool did the double, winning the League Championship and defeating Everton 3-1 in the FA Cup Final. However, it could have been a different story. For after Gary Lineker had given the Blues the lead, it was only Molby's tremendous passing ability that turned the game round as he picked out Ian Rush for the equaliser and Craig Johnston for the second Liverpool goal. The following season he was an important member of the Liverpool side that finished runners-up in the First Division and were beaten 2-1 by Arsenal in the League Cup Final.

In 1987-88 Molby made just one full League appearance as he suffered from a spate of injuries, though he did come on as a substitute in the losing FA Cup Final against Wimbledon. He also missed much of the following season after being jailed for three months on a drink-driving conviction.

Although he won a second League Championship medal in 1989-90, Molby made only 12 appearances. After that he began to lose his way somewhat, because of both weight and injury problems, and he found himself playing second fiddle to both Steve McMahon and Ronnie Whelan in the Liverpool midfield. Even when he did return, his lack of mobility regularly found him caught in possession. However, when the Dane was given time and space he could direct operations as he did to great effect in the 1992 FA Cup Final against Sunderland when he created all the Reds' second-half chances.

Midway through the following season, an ankle injury in the match against Manchester United forced Molby to have a six-month lay-off. He made his return as a substitute at Anfield in the Everton derby game, only to aggravate his hamstring and be sidelined to the end of the season. Though there was talk of a possible move to Tranmere Rovers, Molby remained at Anfield, looking his usual calm and elegant self whenever he was called upon by Liverpool.

During the 1995-96 season, Molby was loaned out to both Barnsley and Norwich City before deciding on a move to Swansea City to become the Welsh club's player-manager.

Although the Swans were ultimately relegated, the Dane's pedigree stood out whether in midfield or defence and in 1996-97 he was included in the Third Division PFA side as he led the Vetch Field club to the play-offs. Surprisingly sacked in October 1997, Molby joined Kidderminster Harriers, leading them into the Football League after winning the Conference title.

Honours
League Championship
1985-86, 1989-90
FA Cup
1985-86, 1991-92
League Cup 1994-95
67 Denmark caps

RONNIE MORAN

Born	28 February 1934
Birthplace	Liverpool
Height	5ft 9 ins
Weight	13 st 2 lbs

Team	Apps	Gls
Liverpool	343	14

One of the finest servants Liverpool Football Club has ever known, Ronnie Moran has been associated with the club in almost every capacity. He came to Anfield as a 17-year-old in 1951, making his League debut for an indifferent Liverpool side at Derby County in November 1952. However, he was unable to claim a regular place during the Reds' two-year struggle against relegation which ended unsuccessfully at the end of the 1953-54 season. He established himself in the Liverpool side midway through the following season as a replacement for Frank Lord. Over the next five seasons, Moran missed just six league matches and enjoyed a spell as captain at the end of the decade as the Reds tried desperately to regain their top flight status.

One of Moran's best games during this period as against Bristol Rovers at Eastville in December 1959. The home side were dominating the game and threatening to overrun the Reds' defence but Moran who made three goal-line clearances and a number of last ditch tackles, stood firm. Liverpool went on to win 2-0 with two breakaway goals - a victory that was largely won by their popular left-back.

In the early part of the 1960s, Moran underwent sixteen months of injury problems, making just a handful of appearances. With promotion finally beckoning, it seemed that he would miss out on the triumph but thankfully he returned to full fitness to help the club win the Second Division Championship in 1961-62.

In the Reds' second season back in the top flight, Ronnie Moran played in 35 league games as they lifted

in the 1965 FA Cup Final, Gerry Byrne broke his collarbone and Ronnie Moran was called up to do battle in the two-legged European Cup semi-final against Inter Milan. Despite Moran giving a good account of himself against the brilliant Brazilian Jair, the Reds lost 4-3 on aggregate, even though they had won the first leg at Anfield 3-1.

Moran then retired to the Liverpool bootroom, becoming the club's reserve team trainer in 1972 and later first-team coach. As Joe Fagan's number two, many expected him to take over when Fagan retired but instead he was overlooked in favour of Kenny Dalglish. When Dalglish resigned as manager in February 1991, Moran temporarily took control but a poor run of results not only cost Liverpool the title but almost certainly cost Moran the chance of becoming manager.

There is no doubt that Ronnie Moran's inspired backroom work as the Reds evolved into one of the dominant powers in British football has tended to overshadow his playing career but the burly full-back was also one of the game's best uncapped defenders.

the League Championship. However, the strong, sturdy defender was now beginning to slow down and midway through the 1964-65 season, Chris Lawler came into the side at right-back with Gerry Byrne switching to Ronnie Moran's left-back spot.

When Liverpool beat Leeds United

Honours
League Championship
1963-64
Second Division Championship
1961-62

PHIL NEAL

Born	20 February 1951
Birthplace	Irchester
Height	5ft 11ins
Weight	12st 2lbs

Team	Apps	Gls
Northampton T	183 (4)	28
Liverpool	453 (2)	41
Bolton W.	56 (8)	3

Phil Neal began his career with Northampton Town and had made 206 appearances for the Cobblers when Bob Paisley bought him for £65,000 in October 1974. He made his debut for the Reds against Everton the following month as a replacement for the injured Alec Lindsay at left-back.

He was ever-present from his second appearance for the club in December 1974 until he missed a defeat against Sunderland in October 1983 - a run of 366 consecutive League matches, mostly in the No2 shirt.

An intelligent, positional player, Neal denied the winger any space. Though he was excellent in defence, his distribution was immaculate. The majority of his goals came from the penalty-spot, Phil taking this role from Kevin Keegan in his second season. He hit the clincher in the 1977 European Cup Final from the spot and was on the mark again against AS Roma in 1984. He played in a total of four European Cup Finals, captaining the club in two of them.

His masterly performances at full-back week in, week out, were an integral part of the Reds' great defensive displays over the years. When he was forced to miss the second leg of a European Cup tie against Odense, it ended a club record 417 consecutive appearances.

Neal won almost every honour while playing for Liverpool, picking up eight League Championship medals, he was also on the winning side in four League Cup Finals. He won a UEFA Cup winners' medal and four European Cup winners' medals - only an FA Cup winners' medal eluded him. He is the most capped England right-back of all-time with 50 caps to his name. His last appearance was against Denmark at Wembley in September 1983.

Neal succeeded Graeme Souness as skipper for the 1984-85 season but halfway through the following campaign he left to join Bolton Wanderers as player-manager. He had made 635 first team appearances for Liverpool and scored 60 goals.

At Bolton he continued to play, lending his experience to the younger players. His first few years in management were quite eventful. He led the side to Wembley where they lost 3-0 to Bristol City in the Freight Rover Trophy Final. The club were relegated to the Fourth Division for the first time in their history but bounced back immediately at the end of the following campaign. There was another visit to Wembley in 1989, Bolton beating Torquay United 4-1 to win the Sherpa Van Trophy.

On leaving Burnden Park, Neal had a period of involvement with the England management team before taking charge of Coventry City in November 1993. His appointment helped to steady the team and they finished the season in mid-table. However, midway through the following campaign, the Sky Blues failed to beat a number of fellow strugglers and in February 1995, this led to the departure of Neal by mutual consent. A year later he took charge of Cardiff City before spending a brief spell as caretaker-manager of Manchester City.

Honours
League Championship
1975-76, 1976-77, 1978-79, 1979-80, 1981-82, 1982-83, 1983-84, 1985-86
League Cup
1980-81, 1981-82, 1982-83, 1983-84
European Cup
1976-77, 1977-78, 1980-81, 1983-84
UEFA Cup 1975-76
50 England caps

STEVE NICOL

	Born	11 December 1961
	Birthplace	Irvine
	Height	5ft 10ins
	Weight	12st 6lbs

Team	Apps	Gls
Liverpool	328 (15)	36
Notts Co.	32	2
Sheff Wed.	41 (8)	0
West Brom	9	0

Before coming south to join Liverpool in October 1981, Steve Nicol had spent just over two seasons with Ayr United, having impressed at full-back after signing from a local boys' club. He had to wait almost a year before making his Football League debut at Birmingham City in August 1982 and made only three more appearances that season, two of them as a substitute, before earning a regular place in the club's midfield the following season.

Replacing the injured Craig Johnston, he ended the 1983-84 campaign with League Championship and European Cup winners' medals. Nicol played on the right side of midfield before taking over the right-back position from Phil Neal in October 1985 but following the signing of Barry Venison, he alternated between full-back and midfield.

Nicol made his international debut for Scotland against Yugoslavia in September 1984, a match the Scots won 6-1, and after playing in the 1986 World Cup Finals he became a fairly regular selection for the next seven years.

In September 1987 Nicol scored his first and only senior hat-trick as the Reds won 4-1 at Newcastle United. In 1988-89 he was switched to central defence after both Gary Gillespie and Alan Hansen were injured and he performed so well in this emergency role, that he was voted the Football Writers' Association Footballer of the Year in 1989.

Injuries hampered his progress over the next couple of seasons but in 1991-92 Nicol was one of few senior players at Anfield to escape long-term injury. He began the season at right-back but switched to midfield after the

emergence of Rob Jones and then to central defence to cover the absence of Nicky Tanner, but reverted to full-back to win his third FA Cup winners' medal at the end of the season.

Nicol was an innocent victim of the constant 'club versus country' tug-of-war between Liverpool and Scotland, and in September 1991 he made his 27th and final appearance for his country against Switzerland. Nicol played a full part in the Reds' almost unbroken run of success, winning four League Championship medals and three FA Cup winners' medals plus a losers' medal in 1988.

On being given a free transfer by Liverpool, Nicol joined Notts County where he continued to be recognised as a player who could carry his competitiveness and skill to any position. He became part of the club's management team alongside Wayne Jones for the last seven games of the 1994-95 season.

In November 1995, Nicol joined Sheffield Wednesday and, with the side struggling, it seemed that a position in the back four or just in front of them best suited him, but he also had to play in midfield. A great calming influence on the younger players in the Wednesday side, he let neither himself nor his manager down. He had a brief loan spell with West Bromwich Albion before being released by Wednesday in the summer of 1998.

Honours
League Championship
1983-84, 1985-86,
1987-88, 1989-90
FA Cup 1985-86, 1988-89
European Cup 1983-84
27 Scotland caps

MICHAEL OWEN

Born	14 December 1979
Birthplace	Chester
Height	5ft 9ins
Weight	11st 2lbs

Team	Apps	Gls
Liverpool	167 (20)	102

Michael Owen's name first appeared on a Liverpool team sheet on the day Robbie Fowler scored his 100th goal for the club. It was Owen's 17th birthday and the fact that the Reds were so keen to promote him shows how highly he was rated at Anfield. He eventually made his first-team debut as a substitute for Patrik Berger in a 2-1 defeat at Wimbledon in May 1997, scoring the club's goal when he raced on to Stig Bjornebye's through ball to become Liverpool's youngest-ever scorer.

Playing for Deeside Schools against boys often three years older than himself, Owen beat Ian Rush's record of 72 goals in a season by a clear twenty and went on to pass the previous best for appearances by Gary Speed - scoring 148 goals in 115 games. He broke England's scoring records at both Under-15 and Under-16 levels and hit eleven goals in five games to take the Reds to their first-ever FA Youth Cup success.

Having got his Liverpool career underway in 1996-97, Owen proceeded to embark on his full international career in February 1998 against Chile at Wembley when, at the age of 18 years and 59 days, he became the youngest player of the twentieth century to play for England. It was a magnificent season for the goalscoring wizard, usurping the great heights to which both Fowler and Rush had aspired. He scored 23 goals including hat-tricks in the League Cup against Grimsby Town (home 3-0) and Sheffield Wednesday in the Premiership (away 3-3).

Named as the PFA Young Player of the Year and included in the PFA Premiership selection, Owen was held back during England's opening game of the World Cup Finals against Romania. He was introduced in the 73rd minute and scored an equaliser

the back of the net with regularity but, goalscoring apart, his relentless running in the Liverpool cause destroyed the myth that he had expended too much energy during England's World Cup campaign in France.

A hamstring injury hampered his progress the following season and doubts emerged about his level of fitness and his tendency to break down. However, when he was in the Liverpool team he made a telling contribution. Recovering in time for Euro 2000, he featured in all three of England's matches, scoring in the final game against Romania before the Romanians snatched a last-minute winner, even then 'Boy Wonder' nearly equalized in the dying moments when he struck a post.

Nevertheless Owen showed his true worth against Argentina when he raced past two defenders to shoot across the keeper for one of the goals of the competition. Although England went out following a penalty shoot-out, he was acknowledged by all as a future 'great'.

The 1998-99 season was yet another spectacular one for Michael Owen. After a brilliant hat-trick in a 4-1 win at Newcastle United in the third game of the campaign, he continued to hit

The club's leading league goalscorer in 2000-01, Owen rewrote Liverpool's FA Cup history when he grabbed two goals in the last seven minutes to turn the final around and steal the trophy from Arsenal who had dominated the game but failed to put away their chances. Owen's double strikes were true class in the first FA Cup Final to be played at Cardiff's Millennium Stadium.

He started the last season in fine style, notching a hat-trick for England in a 5-1 win in Germany and helping his country reach the World Cup Finals where goals against Denmark and Brazil further enhanced his reputation as a finisher of the highest class.

Honours
FA Cup 2000-01
League Cup 2000-01, 2002-03
UEFA Cup 2000-01
40 England caps

JAMIE REDKNAPP

Born	25 June 1973
Birthplace	Barton-on-Sea
Height	6ft 0ins
Weight	12st 10lbs

Team	Apps	Gls
Bournemouth	6 (7)	0
Liverpool	207 (30)	30
Tottenham H.	14 (3)	3

The son of former West Ham United manager Harry Redknapp, Jamie was courted by Tottenham Hotspur as an associated schoolboy but on leaving school, he joined his father who was then managing Bournemouth. He made his Football League debut at Hull City in January 1990 at the age of 16 years 202 days before turning professional in the summer on his 17th birthday.

Clearly a player of great potential, Redknapp's name was already being mentioned as a target for bigger clubs and although not a first-team regular at Dean Court, he was signed by Liverpool in January 1991 as an investment for the future. He received a first team opportunity earlier than expected because of Liverpool's long injury list and he made his debut in the UEFA Cup tie away to Auxerre which the Reds lost 2-0, although they overturned the deficit in the second leg. His League debut for the club came at Southampton in December 1991 when he scored the equaliser after coming on as a substitute. Further opportunities came his way later in the season but he played no part in the later stages of the Reds' FA Cup run.

Replacing the injured Paul Stewart, Redknapp was Liverpool's major discovery of 1992-93, holding his place until the return of Ronnie Whelan in March 1993. He gave an outstanding display against Spartak Moscow in the European Cup Winners' Cup but was sent off for a second bookable offence in the 5-1 debacle at Coventry City after scoring from a superb free-kick. That season also saw him make a scoring debut for the England Under-21 side against San Marino, before becoming a regular selection.

Redknapp won his first honour with the club in 1995 as Steve McManaman netted both the Reds' goals in a 2-1 Coca Cola Cup Final win over Bolton Wanderers. In 1995-96 he was playing to the peak of his ability in the Reds' midfield, displaying magnificent control and passing skills and scoring spectacular goals against Vladikavkaz in the UEFA Cup and Blackburn Rovers. He seemed certain to establish himself in the England side but then suffered a serious injury in the early stages of the international against Switzerland. Even after recovering, he spent several weeks on the bench as Roy Evans chose not to change a winning team. He was eventually restored to first-team duty for the FA Cup semi-final against Aston Villa and then came back for England in Euro 96.

Injuries and the form of Michael Thomas restricted Redknapp's appearances until late in the season in 1996-97. The following season he was a major influence on the Liverpool side - indeed, the Reds seemed to struggle without him.

He married the pop star Louise in the summer of 1998 and had a super season with Liverpool in 1998-99, with his best performance coming against Manchester United. He continued to feature in successive England managers' plans until another injury to his knee and subsequent cartilage operation robbed them and Liverpool of his services for much of the last few seasons. In fact, Redknapp didn't appear at all in the first team in 2000-01. As Liverpool rediscovered their winning ways, Jamie found opportunities at the club limited and was sold to Tottenham Hotspur before the current season.

Honours
League Cup 1994-95
17 England caps

IAN RUSH

Born	20 October 1961	
Birthplace	St. Asaph	
Height	6ft 0ins	
Weight	12st 6lbs	

Team	Apps	Gls
Chester City	33 (1)	14
Liverpool	447 (22)	229
Leeds United	34 (2)	3
Newcastle Utd	6 (4)	0
Sheff Wed (L)	4	0
Wrexham	12 (5)	0

After Bob Paisley paid Chester City £30,000 for the services of Ian Rush in May 1980, many doubted the shrewdness of this acquisition as Rush struggled to find the net in Central League games. In fact, there was even talk of him moving on, but Liverpool took care not to rush him. He became a full international over six months before his first team debut for Liverpool, which came towards the end of the 1980-81 season.

In 1981-82 Rush scored 30 goals in 49 games, winning his first League Championship medal in the process. There were further League titles in 1982-83 and 1983-84, European Cup victory in 1984 and League Cup wins in 1982-83 and 1983-84. The derby game with Everton in November 1982 saw Liverpool beat the Blues 5-0 at Goodison with Rush netting four.

The following season Rush won the Golden Boot Award with 32 goals scored in Division One matches. Unlike the run-of-the-mill strikers, Rush was the focal point of the Liverpool attacks, collecting the ball out of defence and laying it off simply but effectively before speeding off to a new position. The sight of him breaking free to leave defenders in his wake before slotting the ball home is one that lingers long in the memory.

Perhaps the peak of his career came in 1985-86 when the Reds lifted the near impossible League and Cup double, with Rush scoring twice in the 3-1 FA Cup Final victory over Everton.

Rush deeply appreciated being voted Player of the Year in 1984. Liverpool's dependence on Rush's flow of goals was shown by the run of 144 matches in which the side never lost when he scored. That record was broken when his 202nd goal was beaten by two from Charlie Nicholas as Arsenal won the 1987 Littlewoods Cup.

Rush's reputation as one of the world's great strikers had clubs battling for his signature. Eventually Juventus succeeded in a deal worth

£3.2 million. There was one consolation for the Anfield faithful in that he would be staying for one more season. Rush showed his greatness by playing his heart out and scoring 30 goals in 42 league games. He ended the season in style, hitting two goals in a 3-1 win over Everton, bringing his tally in derby matches to 19, equalling Dixie Dean's record.

Following an unhappy time in Italy, Rush returned to the Anfield fold in a sensational £2.8 million transfer just before the start of the 1988-89 season. Coming on as substitute in the 1989 FA Cup Final against Everton, Rush scored two goals as Liverpool won 3-2 after extra time, taking his total of derby goals to 21 to pass Dixie Dean's record of long ago. Towards the end of his Liverpool career he became the club captain and while he continued to score goals, he found time to coach the young Robbie Fowler.

One of Liverpool's finest-ever players, having scored 306 goals in 602 games, Rush joined Leeds United in May 1997. At Elland Road he hit the worst goalscoring drought of his long career and at the end of the season he joined Newcastle United. With the Magpies he extended his record as the top FA Cup goalscorer of the twentieth century before, following a loan spell with Sheffield United, he joined Wrexham as their player-coach. Surprisingly he left the Racecourse Ground the following summer.

Honours
League Championship
1981-82, 1982-83, 1983-84,
1985-86, 1989-90
FA Cup 1985-86, 1988-89
League Cup
1980-81, 1981-82
1982-83, 1983-84, 1994-95
European Cup
1983-84
73 Wales caps

IAN ST JOHN

Born	7 June 1938	
Birthplace	Motherwell	
Height	5ft 7ins	
Weight	11st 6lbs	

Team	Apps	Gls
Liverpool	334 (2)	95
Coventry City	18	3
Tranmere R	9	1

After paying Motherwell £37,500 for the Saint, Bill Shankly described him as the man the Reds couldn't afford not to buy, the most urgently needed component of his new team. In 1959 while playing for the Fir Park Club, he set a new record for the fastest hat-trick in Scottish football, netting three goals in the space of two-and-a-half minutes! His first appearance in a red shirt was in a Liverpool Senior Cup Final against Everton at Goodison Park in August 1961 - he was an instant hit with the fans as he scored a hat-trick.

St John was strong, courageous and quite devastating in the air for a man of 5ft 7ins. His delicate flicks did much to promote a fine understanding with Roger Hunt - he scored 18 goals that first season as the Reds won promotion. During that Division Two title campaign, St John often showed flashes of bad temper and in March 1962 he was sent off along with Preston's Tony Singleton after such a clash. Fire, though, was an integral part of the Saint's make-up

St John's first season in the top flight saw him score 19 goals and then 21 in 1963-64 as Liverpool went on to win the Championship. During that successful campaign, Jimmy Melia, Liverpool's scheming inside-forward, was injured and Shanks withdrew St John into a deep-lying role. He showed his true potential and became the mastermind of the Reds' attack. He gave his team-mates plenty of possession and created space for them with his intelligent running. It certainly wasn't the end of his goals, his jack-knife header against Leeds United at Wembley in 1965 winning the FA Cup.

Roger Hunt would be the first to admit that he benefited greatly from St John's talents as he readily acknowledged after the 1965 European Cup Winners' Cup-tie against Standard Liege. After running half the length of the field, drawing defenders with him, St John slipped the ball through to an

unmarked Hunt to score.

As his fitness began to decline, St John was used a little more sparingly. On the substitutes' bench for the European fairs Cup-tie against Dynamo Bucharest, he was brought into the game with Liverpool holding a precarious 1-0 lead. With his touch and close passing skills, he laid on two goals near the end of the match to leave the Reds comfortable winners at 3-0.

The Saint was a tough and tenacious player, representing Scotland on 21 occasions.

On leaving Anfield he had short spells with Coventry City and Tranmere Rovers before trying coaching and then management. He didn't succeed as many people thought he might and eventually he became a TV personality, sharing the screen with another great goalscorer from the 1960s, Jimmy Greaves.

However, it is not as Greavsie's chat-show partner that the Saint should be recalled but as the first piece of the Liverpool jigsaw that has seen success over the last four decades.

Honours
League Championship
1963-64, 1965-66
Second Division Championship
1961-62
FA Cup 1964-65
21 Scotland caps

TOMMY SMITH

Born	5 April 1945
Birthplace	Liverpool
Height	5ft 10ins
Weight	11st 7lbs

Team	Apps	Gls
Liverpool	467	36
Swansea City	34 (2)	2

Born within a corner kick's distance of Anfield, Tommy Smith grew up to become one of the club's greatest servants. He developed into one of the toughest defenders in the Football League and was club captain for a while. Smith made his Liverpool debut against Birmingham City in May 1963, standing in for the injured Gordon Milne. In his reserve days at Anfield, it was rumoured that he was a target for Manchester United but nothing came of it.

Tommy Smith quickly became an integral member of Bill Shankly's first great Liverpool side. He had two roles, initially in midfield before moving into the centre of defence. His game boasted more skill than it was given credit for and Smith contributed greatly to Liverpool's FA Cup success of 1965 and the ensuing Championship campaign.

When Smith moved into defence, Bill Shankly told him 'Think of yourself as Ron Yeats' right leg' and he developed into a player of great authority. He was the obvious choice to succeed the big Scotsman as captain, which he did in March 1970.

As a leader, Smith was an inspiration, driving the team on to greater effort. He relished the position and its responsibilities and in the 1970-71 season gave some of his best-ever performances. He won his only England cap and was only just pipped as 'Footballer of the Year' by Arsenal's Frank McLintock. He led Liverpool to the FA Cup Final in 1971 when they lost to Arsenal before leading the Reds to a unique double of League Championship and UEFA Cup in 1972-73.

After being dropped in November 1973, he had heated words with Bill Shankly, the confrontation losing him the captaincy to Emlyn Hughes. He almost moved to Stoke City but returned to the side to replace the injured Chris Lawler at right-back. After winning more trophies and troubled by knee problems, he announced his retirement in early 1977.

However, Phil Thompson was injured and Smith found himself back in the centre of defence. He had a superb season, facing Manchester United at Wembley in the FA Cup Final, winning another League Championship medal and then making his 600th appearance in a Liverpool shirt in the European Cup Final against Borussia Moenchengladbach. To cap it all, the veteran of so many past glories rose majestically to meet Heighway's corner to send a header of immense power crashing into the Germans' net.

He stayed at Anfield for another season and would probably have played against Bruges in the European Cup Final but dropped a pickaxe on his foot!

Though he was offered a one-year contract, Smith joined John Toshack at Swansea, after the latter made him a better offer. He later made a brief Anfield return as coach.

A player of great courage, toughness and determination, he will go down in folklore as one of the hardest men the game has known. For his services to the game, he was awarded the MBE in 1976.

Honours
League Championship
1965-66, 1972-73, 1975-76
1976-77
FA Cup 1964-65, 1973-74
European Cup
1976-77
UEFA Cup
1972-73, 1975-76
1 England cap

GRAEME SOUNESS

Born	6 May 1953
Birthplace	Edinburgh
Height	5ft 11ins
Weight	12st 13lbs

Team	Apps	Gls
Middlesbrough	174 (2)	22
Liverpool	246 (1)	38

Throughout his career, Graeme Souness has exhibited a fierce desire to succeed but with established midfielders of the quality of Mullery, Peters and Perryman at White Hart Lane, the young Souness grew frustrated. After playing for Montreal Olympic in the NASL in the summer of 1972, he walked out on the club before Spurs allowed him to move to Middlesbrough for £32,000.

At the end of his first season at Ayresome Park, Middlesbrough were promoted to Division One and during his stay in the north-east, Souness developed into one of the game's most influential performers of modern times.

It was Bob Paisley who brought Souness to Anfield in January 1978 for £352,000 - then a record deal between Football League clubs. His move to Liverpool to team up with Kenny Dalglish was the foundation stone of the club's success over the next decade. The two dovetailed perfectly and Souness provided the pass for Dalglish to score the winning goal against Bruges in the 1978 European Cup Final. There were occasions when his tackling provoked resentment from opponents, but Souness was to stamp his influence on crucial matches for both Liverpool and Scotland.

His displays in the European Cup campaign of 1980-81 were particularly eye-catching, with his sense of awareness and ability to rip open the hearts of defences with long, telling passes. He also hit two hat-tricks in the early stages of the competition as Liverpool beat Oulu Palloseura of Finland 10-1 and CSKA Sofia of Bulgaria 5-1 in the Anfield legs.

In March 1982 Spurs felt the full force of Souness when he came on as substitute (the only time he was a substitute at Anfield) with the Reds 2-0 down. He was returning after a back injury and helped pull the game round, the final score being 2-2.

He scored some valuable goals for Liverpool, none more so perhaps than the one that beat Everton in the 1984

Milk Cup Final replay. Replacing Phil Thompson as captain, he led the Reds to three successive League titles and League Cups and one European Cup, becoming the most successful skipper in the club's history.

In June 1984 he moved to Sampdoria in Italy for £650,000. Two quiet seasons were followed by his surprise appointment as player-manager at Ibrox in 1986.

In his first game for Rangers he was sent off! However by the end of his first season, the club had won the Scottish League and the Skol Cup and reached the final of the Scottish Cup while in 1989-90 they won the Scottish League title again and in 1990-91 the Skol Cup. A part-owner of Rangers, Souness was still striving for the European Champions Cup when he left in April 1991 to replace former Anfield team-mate Kenny Dalglish as manager of Liverpool.

In his first season, Souness made many expensive changes and after the shock of undergoing major heart surgery, he led the Reds to the one trophy he had failed to capture as a player, the FA Cup. However in January 1994 Souness resigned his post. He then spent a season in Turkey with Galatasaray but was sacked after winning the Championship. In July 1996 he was appointed manager of Southampton but after one season he resigned following a disagreement about money for new players. After a spell managing Serie 'B' club Torino, Souness took charge of Blackburn Rovers and having led them to promotion to the Premiership in 2000-01, saw Rovers win the League Cup at Cardiff's Millennium Stadium in 2001.

Honours
League Championship
1978-79, 1979-80, 1981-82, 1982-83, 1983-84
League Cup
1980-81, 1981-82, 1982-83, 1983-84
European Cup
1977-78, 1980-81, 1983-84
54 Scotland caps

PETER THOMPSON

Born	27 November 1942
Birthplace	Carlisle
Height	5ft 8ins
Weight	11st 6lbs

Team	Apps	Gls
Preston NE	121	20
Liverpool	318 (4)	41
Bolton W	111 (6)	2

Peter Thompson began his career with Preston North End, turning professional the year the legendary Tom Finney retired. He soon established himself as one of Preston's most consistent performers and in August 1963, in the face of opposition from Everton, Wolves and Juventus, Bill Shankly paid £40,000 to bring him to Anfield. The day he signed for Liverpool, Shankly told him he'd be the best player in the world, the fastest thing on two legs and that he would become the 'White Pele'.

After an impressive debut against Blackburn Rovers at Ewood Park, where he forced the Rovers' defenders to twist and turn in their efforts to stay with him, Thompson became a great favourite with the Reds' supporters. At the end of his first full season, Liverpool won the League Championship and Thompson gave his best display of the campaign in a 5-0 rout of Arsenal, scoring twice as the Reds made certain of the title.

There were those who said he should score more goals. When he did score, they were often spectacular and match-winners. In the 1964-65 FA Cup semi-final against Chelsea, he waltzed past Hinton and Hollins to hit a superb left-footer out of Bonetti's reach.

The accuracy of Thompson's crosses played an important part in establishing Roger Hunt as one of the most feared goalscorers of the time and in 1965-66 it was no coincidence that Thompson played in 40 games and Hunt scored 27 goals.

Making his international debut against Portugal in 1964, Thompson was a regular in the England side for the next two years, though he was a victim of Alf Ramsey's decision to play the 1966 World Cup without wingers. He played in the 2-1 win over Northern Ireland at Wembley in

November 1965 but in the next match against Spain, Alan Ball wore the No.7 shirt. The last of Thompson's 16 caps came against Scotland in 1970.

Peter Thompson was a fantastic winger; he could take on defenders in tight situations, go past them with ease and had great speed and superb ball control. He collected two League Championship medals and an FA Cup winners' medal with Liverpool.

However, after being plagued by knee trouble, Thompson found himself languishing in the Reds' reserve side and in November 1973 he moved to Bolton Wanderers on loan. Though he had been considering retirement, he made his debut for the Wanderers against Second Division leaders Sunderland in a game played on a Wednesday afternoon because of the power strike. Bolton won 1-0, the fans took him to their hearts immediately and in January 1974 he signed for the Trotters for £18,000 - one of the bargain buys of all-time. His displays on the wing helped Bolton through one of their most exciting periods and to promotion to Division One.

Thompson, who remains one of the Liverpool folk heroes, retired in April 1978 and after running a caravan park, now runs a hotel in Harrogate.

Honours
League Championship
1963-64, 1965-66
FA Cup 1964-65
16 England caps

PHIL THOMPSON

Born	21 January 1954
Birthplace	Liverpool
Height	6ft 0ins
Weight	11st 8lbs

Team	Apps	Gls
Liverpool	337 (3)	7
Sheffield Utd	36 (1)	0

As a youngster, Phil Thompson stood on the Kop to cheer his favourites, so it was a dream come true when he actually signed on at Anfield. Bill Shankly used to say about Thompson: 'He's tossed up with a sparrow for legs and lost.' Thompson's frail-looking frame gave the impression that he wouldn't make a top-class defender because he lacked the necessary physical attributes. This couldn't be further from the truth for Phil's determination and skill earned him the captaincy of both Liverpool and England.

Originally a midfielder, Thompson made his debut for Liverpool as a substitute at Old Trafford in April 1972. The following season he went on to play in enough matches in a variety of positions to qualify for a League Championship medal. Bill Shankly however spotted potential in Thompson in a different role. With regular centre-back Larry Lloyd injured, it was Thompson that Shanks turned to as Emlyn Hughes' partner.

In the 1974 FA Cup Final, Thompson completely shackled the Newcastle United and England centre-forward Malcolm Macdonald as Liverpool ran out 3-0 winners in one of the most one-side post-war finals. The self-styled 'Super Mac' had threatened to bring the Reds' defence to their knees!

The Thompson-Hughes combination grew in authority at the heart of the Reds' defence, it was a partnership that played a great part in Liverpool's success as the trophies piled up during the second-half of the 1970s.

Thompson was a great reader of the game, often playing his way out of trouble in European style, keeping the ball and setting up attacks with superb distribution.

Liverpool often attacked en masse

and it was Thompson who was left at the back ready to deal with any possible breakaways - he was probably the most accomplished British defender in a one-to-one situation. Having said that, it was Phil Thompson who was involved in that televised and much debated League Cup Final replay of 1977-78 against Nottingham Forest. When John O'Hare broke away, Thompson chased after him and brought him down just outside the area but despite Liverpool's strong protests, the referee awarded a penalty and John Robertson tucked it away.

When Emlyn Hughes relinquished his place in the Liverpool side to Alan Hansen, it was Phil Thompson who took over the captaincy. He was a great motivator, inspiring his team-mates to new heights. As captain, he led the Reds to two League Championships and European Cup success over Real Madrid in 1981. He played 42 times for England with a stint as captain.

At Anfield, Graeme Souness became captain but Thompson played on and won two further League Championship medals. Thompson's career on Merseyside came to an end in 1985 after being hit by a crop of injuries. He moved on to Sheffield United but wasn't away for long for, eighteen months later, he was invited back to Anfield as a member of the coaching staff.

Later a pundit for Sky TV, Thompson, one of the Kop's greatest sons, is back at Anfield as assistant manager to Gerard Houllier.

Honours
League Championship
1975-76, 1978-79, 1979-80,
1981-82, 1982-83
FA Cup 1973-74
League Cup
1980-81, 1981-82
European Cup
1977-78, 1980-81
UEFA Cup 1975-76
42 England caps

JOHN TOSHACK

Born	22 March 1949
Birthplace	Cardiff
Height	6ft 1ins
Weight	12st 0lbs

Team	Apps	Gls
Cardiff City	159 (3)	75
Liverpool	169 (3)	74
Swansea City	58 (5)	24

John Toshack shared an interest and ability in cricket as well as football and it is perhaps not too surprising to discover that Ernie Toshack, an Australian Test cricketer, is a distant relative. However, though he played cricket for the Welsh Schoolboys XI, Toshack's first love was football and on leaving school he joined Cardiff City as an apprentice. He broke into the Bluebirds' first team in 1965-66, when at the age of 16 years 236 days he scored the final goal in a 3-1 win over Leyton Orient.

Toshack continued to find the net over the next few seasons and in 1968-69 was the Second Division's leading scorer. By the time he left Ninian Park to sign for Liverpool for £110,000 in November 1970, he had scored 100 goals in 203 games and was already a Welsh international, having been capped against Scotland in 1969. He

won over the Reds' fans immediately, for in the derby game with Everton he turned things round after Liverpool had gone 2-0 down. He scored Liverpool's equalising goal, climbing high above Brian Labone to power in a ferocious header and then nodding down an Alec Lindsay cross for full-back Chris Lawler to clinch a 3-2 victory.

Toshack's most prolific season was 1975-76 when he scored 23 goals including three hat-tricks, as Liverpool won the League Championship and the UEFA Cup. In his seven seasons at Liverpool, he scored 95 goals in 236 games. It was his heading ability that won him the most of his accolades, gaining a reputation for scoring with far post headers, though to be fair, he also possessed a deceptively neat touch on the ground. The partnership he established with Kevin Keegan made the pair of them the most feared attacking force in the First Division. They were almost impossible to contain, some pressmen claiming that they had some kind of telepathic understanding!

For most of his Anfield career, Toshack was dogged by a nagging thigh injury and indeed only once did he exceed 30 league games in a season. In March 1978, even though a host of English and foreign clubs were trying to sign him, Liverpool let him go on a free transfer to become player-manager of Swansea City.

He scored on his debut for the Swans, helping the club clinch third place and promotion to Division Three. In a three-year spell with Toshack as their manager, Swansea climbed from the Fourth to the First Division - a feat unrivalled in Football League history. Sadly it all went wrong for Toshack as the Welsh club had debts of more than £1 million from his spending in the transfer market and the team began to disintegrate at an alarming rate.

He resigned with eighteen months of his contract still to run and asked for no compensation. He returned eight weeks later but couldn't halt the slide and was sacked.

After managing Sporting Lisbon, he bounced back in 1986 as manager at Real Sociedad, winning the Spanish Cup by beating Athletico Madrid in his first season. He then took charge of the mighty Real Madrid, winning the Championship in his first season. Despite this, the club sacked him shortly afterwards and in 1991 he returned to Real Sociedad as General Manager.

In March 1994 a spell as Welsh national team manager lasted a mere 44 days and one game before he returned to Spain to take over at Deportivo La Coruna.

Honours
League Championship
1972-73, 1975-76, 1976-77
FA Cup 1973-74
UEFA Cup 1972-73, 1975-76
40 Wales caps

RONNIE WHELAN

Born	23 September 1941
Birthplace	Dublin
Height	5ft 9ins
Weight	12st 3lbs

Team	Apps	Gls
Liverpool	351 (11)	46
Southend Utd	34	1

The son of a former international, who never played in the Football League, Ronnie Whelan was spotted by Liverpool playing in the League of Ireland team Home Farm and was brought to Anfield in October 1979. He had to wait eighteen months before making his Liverpool debut, replacing the injured Ray Kennedy against Stoke City in April 1981 and scoring a goal in a 3-0 win.

The following season Whelan won a regular place in the Liverpool side, scoring 10 League goals and two in the 1982 League Cup Final as the Reds beat Tottenham Hotspur 3-1 after extra-time. In 1983 he popped up again to score the winner in extra-time as Liverpool retained the trophy by beating Manchester United 2-1. After these early exploits, Whelan became an infrequent scorer, though he did score a hat-trick in April 1986 as the Reds beat Coventry City 5-0.

A Republic of Ireland international, 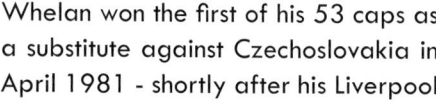 Whelan won the first of his 53 caps as a substitute against Czechoslovakia in April 1981 - shortly after his Liverpool debut. Selected for both the European Championship Finals in West Germany in 1988 and World Cup Finals in Italy in 1990, he will always be remembered for his bicycle-kick volley against the Soviet Union in the former competition that was considered to be 'goal of the tournament' until Van Basten's effort in the final. Sadly, troubled by injury, he played little part in the Republic's remarkable progress to the World Cup quarter-finals in Italy.

On his return from the 1990 World Cup Finals, Whelan had two injury-plagued seasons before returning to first-team action at the beginning of the 1992-93 season. However, he was later withdrawn with a thigh injury and was out for so long that many Liverpool supporters feared that it was one setback too many and that he would

Championship medals, two FA Cup winners' medals and a European Cup winners' medal.

An inspiration to all around him at Roots Hall, Whelan's arrival coincided with a distinct upturn in form and when a groin operation caused him to miss five weeks during January and February 1995, the team's form slumped. Following Steve Thompson's departure, he was appointed the Shrimps' player-manager but a serious knee injury which restricted him to just one appearance in 1995-96, finally forced him to give up the playing side of the game.

Sadly, things started to go wrong for him after he hung up his boots and in February 1997 the club suspended him from team manager duties after an incident with match officials in the Shrimps 3-0 defeat at Manchester City. He was eventually replaced by Alvin Martin.

never play again. Happily he returned to duty in March 1993 and in the nine games he played, Liverpool won six and drew two, finishing the season in sixth place instead of being involved in a mad scramble to avoid relegation. After one more season at Anfield, he left the Reds to join Southend United. Despite an Anfield career riddled with injury, Whelan had won six League

Honours
League Championship
1981-82, 1982-83, 1983-84, 1985-86, 1987-88, 1989-90
FA Cup 1985-86, 1988-89
League Cup
1981-82, 1982-83, 1983-84
European Cup 1983-84
53 Republic of Ireland caps

MARK WRIGHT

Born	1 August 1963
Birthplace	Dorchester
Height	6ft 2ins
Weight	13st 3lbs

Team	Apps	Gls
Oxford Utd	8 (2)	0
Southampton	170	7
Derby County	144	10
Liverpool	156 (2)	5

Mark Wright signed professional forms for Oxford United on his 17th birthday after playing in the Manor Ground club's youth side but had to wait almost a year before making his Football League debut against Bristol City in October 1981. After just eleven first team games for Oxford, he was used as a 'makeweight' in a complicated deal that took him and Keith Cassells to Southampton in exchange for Trevor Hebberd and George Lawrence.

Wright became a fixture at the heart of the Saints' defence from the start of the 1982-83 season, a campaign in which he was selected for the England Under-21 side. The following season he graduated to the national side, winning his first full cap against Wales at Wrexham in May 1984. He became an England regular the following season but missed the 1986 World Cup Finals in Mexico because of a broken leg suffered in the FA Cup semi-final against Liverpool.

After five seasons on the south coast, he joined Peter Shilton in moving to Derby County as part of Robert Maxwell's drive to establish the Rams as a First Division force. Derby sank to the foot of the First Division, doomed to relegation long before the end of the season. Even Wright wilted under the pressure, notably in a 7-1 home defeat by Liverpool.

During the summer of 1991, Wright was sold along with team-mate Dean Saunders to Liverpool, Wright costing the Reds £2.2 million. After making his debut against Oldham Athletic on the opening day of the 1991-92 season, he was injured in the second game and missed the first three months of the campaign. However, when he returned to the team, he was magnificent and under his influence the side reached the FA Cup Final against Sunderland. No honour was more richly deserved than when he captained the Reds to a 2-0 victory. After a number of defensive debacles the following season, Wright was dropped and rumours were rife on Merseyside of a rift with Souness and an early departure.

Though Wright spent most of the next couple of seasons in the reserves, an injury to John Scales at the start of the 1995-96 season gave him another chance to impress. He was easily the most consistent of the four centre-backs at Roy Evans' disposal and he capped his remarkable comeback with a recall to the England team after four years' absence when selected for the match against Croatia. Sadly, as in earlier major international tournaments, just when he seemed assured of a place in the Euro 96 squad, injury once again sidelined him.

Capped 45 times by England, Wright was by now a regular fixture in the Liverpool side, only missing games when injured. Showing all the form that first took him to Anfield, he went a long way to re-establishing himself as one of the best defenders in the Premiership - so much so that he was elected to the award-winning Premiership side at the PFA annual dinner.

Injuries saw the centre-back have a mixed season in 1997-98 and though age was beginning to count against him, he still looked a class act when wearing the red shirt of Liverpool.

At his best he was a player who always appeared to have plenty of time on the ball. Mark Wright later managed non-League Southport before returning to take charge of his first club Oxford United, albeit briefly.

Honours
FA Cup 1991-92
45 England caps

RON YEATS

Born	15 November 1937	
Birthplace	Aberdeen	
Height	6ft 2ins	
Weight	14st 5lbs	

Team	Apps	Gls
Liverpool	357 (1)	13
Tranmere R	96 (1)	5

Bill Shankly's admiration for the 6ft 2ins Scot dated back to when he was manager of Huddersfield Town. He had attempted to sign Yeats from Dundee United then, but the Yorkshire club could not afford the asking price. When installed at Anfield, Shankly failed in an attempt to bring Jack Charlton from Leeds United, so went to Tannadice and paid £30,000 for the man he knew would be the backbone of his first great side.

Shanks called him 'a colossus in defence' - and the description was an apt one. Within five months of his arrival in the summer of 1961, Yeats had been made skipper. In his first season, the Reds galloped to promotion, few centre-forwards finding a way past him.

In the First Division, Ron Yeats proved to be most dominant in the air, while on the ground his tremendous tackling and sensible distribution went to prove what a great capture he had been. He was an inspiring captain, leading the club to two Championships and a succession of superb European matches.

The 1964-65 FA Cup campaign saw Yeats produce some of his most outstanding performances. In the third round at the Hawthorns, he picked up the ball in his own penalty area when somebody in the crowd blew a whistle. Justice was done when Albion's Bobby Cram blasted the ball high and wide. In the fifth round at Burnden Park, he pulled a muscle after only nine minutes but still went on to

> *"an inspiring captain, leading the club to two Championships and a succession of superb European matches."*

keep Wanderers' Welsh international centre-forward Wyn Davies in check. In the sixth round, he laid on the winner for Roger Hunt and then completely dominated Leeds United and England centre-forward Alan Peacock.

Throughout the sixties, Yeats was still essentially a rugged centre-half but as the decade wore on he grew more accomplished. Off the field he was a great influence on the younger players in the Anfield team and though quietly spoken, his imposing personality made him the ideal choice for dealing with the Liverpool management.

After losing his place to Larry Lloyd, he still contributed a valuable spell at left-back. Nicknamed 'Rowdy' after Clint Eastwood's TV cowboy of that era, he made the short trip to Prenton Park, becoming Tranmere Rovers' player-manager and later manager.

Yeats took many former Anfield men to Prenton Park including Bobby Graham, Ian St John, Willie Stevenson and Tommy Lawrence. Attendances began to soar as interest in the club was revitalised but in April 1975 he was sacked.

He then had spells with Stalybridge Celtic and Barrow before he went into the haulage business and then the catering trade.

A player who will go down in Liverpool folklore, Ron Yeats is now the chief scout for the Reds.

Honours
League Championship
1963-64, 1965-66
FA Cup 1964-65
Second Division Championship
1961-62
2 Scotland caps

The Merseyside Derby League Results 1894 to 2002

Liverpool score first

Year	Goodison Pk	Anfield	Year	Goodison Pk	Anfield
1894-95	0-3	2-2	1950-51	3-1	0-2
1896-97	1-2	0-0	1962-63	2-2	0-0
1897-98	0-3	3-1	1963-64	1-3	2-1
1898-99	2-1	2-0	1964-65	1-2	0-4
1899-1900	2-3	1-2	1965-66	0-0	5-0
1900-01	1-1	1-2	1966-67	1-3	0-0
1901-02	0-4	2-2	1967-68	0-1	1-0
1902-03	1-3	0-0	1968-69	0-0	1-1
1903-04	2-5	2-2	1969-70	3-0	0-2
1905-06	2-4	1-1	1970-71	0-0	3-2
1906-07	0-0	1-2	1971-72	0-1	4-0
1907-08	4-2	0-0	1972-73	2-0	1-0
1908-09	0-5	0-1	1973-74	1-0	0-0
1909-10	3-2	0-1	1974-75	0-0	0-0
1910-11	1-0	0-2	1975-76	0-0	1-0
1911-12	1-2	1-3	1976-77	0-0	3-1
1912-13	2-0	0-2	1977-78	0-1	0-0
1913-14	2-1	1-2	1978-79	0-1	1-1
1914-15	3-1	0-5	1979-80	2-1	2-2
1919-20	0-0	3-1	1980-81	2-2	1-0
1920-21	3-0	1-0	1981-82	3-1	3-1
1921-22	1-1	1-1	1982-83	5-0	0-0
1922-23	1-0	5-1	1983-84	1-1	3-0
1923-24	0-1	1-2	1984-85	0-1	0-1
1924-25	0-1	3-1	1985-86	3-2	0-2
1925-26	3-3	5-1	1986-87	0-0	3-1
1926-27	0-1	1-0	1987-88	0-1	2-0
1927-28	1-1	3-3	1988-89	0-0	1-1
1928-29	0-1	1-2	1989-90	3-1	2-1
1929-30	3-3	0-3	1990-91	3-2	3-1
1931-32	1-2	1-3	1991-92	1-1	3-1
1932-33	1-3	7-4	1992-93	1-2	1-0
1933-34	0-0	3-2	1993-94	0-2	2-1
1934-35	0-1	2-1	1994-95	0-2	0-0
1935-36	0-0	6-0	1995-96	1-1	1-2
1936-37	0-2	3-2	1996-97	1-1	1-1
1937-38	3-1	1-2	1997-98	0-2	1-1
1938-39	1-2	0-3	1998-99	0-0	3-2
1946-47	0-1	0-0	1999-2000	0-0	1-0
1947-48	3-0	4-0	2000-01	3-2	3-1
1948-49	1-1	0-0	2001-02	3-1	1-1
1949-50	0-0	3-1	2002-03	2-1	0-0

Morrissey's Manchester
the essential Smiths Tour
by Phill Gatenby
Foreword by Mick Middles
ISBN: 1901746283 - £5.99 - Paperback
"A tour of the people and places that influenced this most influential of bands"

Starmaker
The untold story of Jimmy Murphy
by Brian Hughes MBE
Foreword by Sir John Charles CBE
Introduction by Nobby Stiles MBE
ISBN: 1901746267 - £16.95 - Hardback
The long anticipated biography of 'the greatest soccer coach ever'

Bobby Murdoch, Different Class
by David Potter
Foreword by Billy McNeill
ISBN: 1901746321 - £10.99 - Paperback
'Bobby was an enormous presence with the Lions'
BILLY McNEILL

Viollet
life of a legendary goalscorer
by Roy Cavanagh & Brian Hughes MBE
Foreword by Sir Bobby Charlton CBE
ISBN: 1901746259 - £16.95 - Hardback
'The Fascinating Biography of a Brilliant Footballer'
PAUL HINCE

Order by Credit Card 0161 872 3319

Denis Law, Hero of the Stretford End
by Brian Hughes MBE
ISBN: 1901746356 - £17.95 - 421 pp
'The Greatest Thing on Two Feet'
BILL SHANKLY

Denis Law was hero and villain all rolled into one. His high-octane performances made him a Boys' Own hero to many. He was a player capable of incredible feats of skill and power - all carried off with the knowing smile and villainous touch of a Piccadilly pickpocket. To Mancunians, this son of an Aberdonian trawlerman became part of the fabric of the city; first as a dynamic frontman for the Blues and later as an all-action hero at Matt Busby's United.

In the latest of his biographies of former United greats, Brian Hughes traces the Scot's transformation from unlikely looking teenage footballer to the world's pre-eminent striker. Law's progress up the football ladder was prolific. The bespectacled youth who joined Huddersfield in 1955 didn't look much like a future world star but Bill Shankly's first reaction to his performances on the pitch were telling - 'he's a terror', said the then Huddersfield boss.

But if Denis' subsequent transfers to Manchester City and later Torino confirmed his status as football's rising star, his arrival at Old Trafford in 1962 confirmed him as a phenomenon. The Reds £115,000 swoop secured a player of huge influence both on and off the pitch. For 11 years his personality dominated the thoughts of United fans as Lawmania gripped the city until his shock transfer to the Blues in 1973.

Thus the stage was set for the ironic denouement in April 1974 - Denis' backheel consigning United to Second Division football and the Law legend to immortality.

'Out of the Void'
The Story of Primal Scream
by Brendan Yates
Published September 2003

ISBN: 1901746364 - £10.99 - 260pp
'From leather-clad rock icons to Ecstasy popping ravers, Primal Scream have appealed too and appalled their following in equal measure'

Order by Credit Card 0161 872 3319